THE WRITING AND PUBLISHING JOURNEY

MARK J. CURRAN

Order this book online at www.trafford.com
or email orders@trafford.com

Most Trafford titles are also available at major online book retailers.

 www.trafford.com

North America & international
toll-free: 844 688 6899 (USA & Canada)
fax: 812 355 4082

Our mission is to efficiently provide the world's finest, most comprehensive book publishing
service, enabling every author to experience success. To find out how to publish your book,
your way, and have it available worldwide, visit us online at www.trafford.com

ISBN: 978-1-6987-1407-3 (sc)
          978-1-6987-1408-0 (e)

Print information available on the last page.

Trafford rev. 02/20/2023

THE WRITING AND PUBLISHING JOURNEY

PREFACE

The idea came on the long morning coffee walk on November 11, 2022.

Tell the story of the genesis of each book: how it came about, why, the endeavor to write it, and the real journey – the process of getting it into print. You could call Part I to come "The Publication Travels," or "Travails." With each book use the color jpeg cover. Tell why I began Trafford. Now, 2023, there are forty – one books published.

TABLE OF CONTENTS

THE BOOKS

Introduction to PART I 1

I. Academic Publications while a professor at Arizona State University

1. "A Literatura de Cordel" 4
2. Jorge Amado e a Literatura de CordelJorge Amado e a Literatura de Cordel 11
3. A Presença de Rodolfo Coelho Cavalcante na Moderna Literatura de Cordel 15
4. Cuíca de Santo Amaro Poeta – Repórter da Bahia 19
5. La Literatura de Cordel Brasileña: Antología Bilingüe 24
6. Cuíca de Santo Amaro – Controvérsia no Cordel 27
7. História do Brasil em Cordel 29
8. Retrato do Brasil em Cordel 35

Introduction to PART II 40

II. Books in Retirement at Trafford Publishing

1. Brazil's Folk Popular Poetry – "A Literatura de Cordel" 41
2. The Farm 45
3. Coming of Age with the Jesuits 50
4. Adventures of a 'Gringo' Researcher in Brazil in the 1960s – In Search of the 'Literatura de Cordel 52
5. Peripécias de um Gringo Pesquisador no Brasil nos Anos 1960 ou à Cata do Cordel 54
6. A Trip to Colombia. Highlights of Its Spanish Colonial Heritage 55
7. Travel, Research and Teaching in Guatemala and Mexico. In Quest of the Pre – Columbian Heritage. Volume I. Guatemala 58

8. Travel, Research and Teaching in Guatemala and Mexico in Quest of the Pre – Columbian Heritage. Volume II. México..61

9. Portrait of Brazil in the Twentieth Century – The Universe of the "Literatura de Cordel."... 64

10. Fifty Years of Research in Brazil – A Photographic Journey......................... 66

11. Travel and Teaching in Portugal and Spain 69

12. Relembrando – a Velha Literatura de Cordel e a Voz dos Poetas......................78

13. It Happened in Brazil – Chronicle of a North American Researcher in Brazil II 81

14. Aconteceu no Brasil – Crônicas de um Pesquisador Norte-Americano no Brasil II 84

15. Diary of a North American Researcher in Brazil III 85

16. Diário de um Pesquisador Norte Americano no Brasil III 94

17. Letters from Brazil a Cultural Historical Narrative Made Fiction.....................95

18. A Professor Takes to the Sea. I...97

19. A Professor Takes to the Sea. II..100

20. Letters from Brazil II – Research, Romance, and Dark Days Ahead 105

21. A Rural Odyssey – Living Can Be Dangerous..107

22. Letters from Brazil III. From Glad Times to Sad Times.............................109

23. A Rural Odyssey II - Abilene - Digging Deeper... 111

24. Around Brazil on the 'International Adventurer' – A Panegyric in Fiction.................. 113

25. Pre – Columbian Mexico. Plans, Pitfalls, and Perils..................................115

26. "Portugal and Spain on the 'International Adventurer.'"............................. 117

27. Rural Odyssey III – Dreams Fulfilled and Back to Abilene........................ 119

28. The Collection...121

29. Letters from Brazil IV...125

30. The Master of the "Literatura de Cordel"...127

31. "Adventure Travel" in Guatemala - The Maya Heritage 129

32. TWO by Mark J. Curran. ASU Days. The Guitars a Music Odyssey........................ 131

33. RURAL ODYSSEY IV – PARALLELS. Abilene – Cowboys – "Cordel.".................. 133

34. The Writing and Publishing Journey 135

Addendum: articles or chapters in books 136

Conclusion 143

INTRODUCTION TO PART I

For Not Being a Writer, I Guess I'm a Writer.

First: I'm not a poet, a novelist, a dramatist, or a writer of literary treatises. I possibly could have been a journalist or historian. Oh, or a professor. I wrote the required academic works – dissertation, research articles, short monographs, and several major books. I did not write literary theory because I am not tuned in to it and am not a "deep thinker" to be able to handle "deep structure" and the like. Thank God.

The Trafford Publishing books came later. They are not all the same. They vary from writing "memory" books of growing up on the farm, study at Jesuit Universities, travel and research quests over fifty years, a return to research topics but now in a more informal "conversational" way, and finally writing and publishing what I taught at Arizona State University for 34 years. A second significant narrative style in the latter Trafford books is a mix of "historical or cultural fiction" based on events from the topics described. This endeavor began with baby steps and perhaps has progressed just a bit further but has been a lot more fun. I have created fictional characters and placed them in interesting places with some surprises.

So, we are ready to begin. This is the story of the origin of each book, how it began, the writing, and in the academic stage, the obstacles overcome and good fortune in publishing it. I shall describe each book's topic and content, but only briefly. It is the story of why, when, and how it came to pass that is most interesting.

PART I

THE ACADEMIC BOOKS

I hate clichés but we cannot escape them. "To be honest," (I was incidentally taught by my American Irish-Catholic mother to never but never lie; "It's a sin and off to confession you go"), these books were done at least initially because of "publish or perish" during my teaching career. Uh oh. Another cliché, I love the Jesuit one: "Publish or Parish." Ha ha. To get the coveted and necessary tenure at Arizona State University and then advance in the Academy (you normally start as Assistant Professor, Tenure Track) with only two possible promotions in your entire academic life, you must be a good academic citizen (serve on endless committees, attend myriad faculty meetings, keep your nose clean, and above all don't fall asleep in the meetings, or be a smart – ass in the same), have a good teaching record and evaluations, but lastly and mainly PUBLISH. I learned early that this was the "ticket."

I was, however, one of the truly fortunate professors because the research topics were from the very beginning of great interest to me and fun to tackle. The publishing, to be sure, was the most difficult part. Brazil's "Popular literature in Verse" or "A Literatura de Cordel" is narrative poetry published in pamphlets or broadsides (perhaps 100,000 titles over 100 years) first in the Northeast of Brazil and then also in major cities like Rio de Janeiro and São Paulo. It's complicated and it's not complicated. I am not telling the whole story here; see other books. These story-poems were the principal entertainment and news source for many Brazilians, and erudite authors often adapted them to their works. As we proceed through the many books about them the reader will garner an appreciation for this sentence. I had to collect the broadsides, study why they existed and what they were and what it meant to Brazil. This meant more than twenty trips to Brazil over the years, from over one year in 1966-1967 for the initial research on a Fulbright-Hays Graduate Study Grant, to many stages of two or three months in the summers away from the classroom to shorter trips for conferences and later, book publishing events. Let's get to the books.

1

"A Literatura de Cordel" [Brazil's Folk Popular Poetry or "String Literature"]
Recife: Universidade Federal de Pernambuco, 1973. 94 pp.

A Literatura de Cordel

In June of 1969 with a rather meager ASU travel grant in hand I returned to Brazil to continue research on "cordel," but more importantly to peddle parts or all my dissertation for publication in Brazil. I was a "rookie" in the business, naïve and only with vague ideas. You turn to what you have, "play with the cards they dealt you;" so it seemed to be a good idea to start in Recife where the major research had taken place and later perhaps secondarily in Rio de Janeiro. I must have translated the dissertation from its original English during that academic year.

A first place of inquiry would be the Instituto Joaquim Nabuco de Pesquisas Sociais in far western Recife. I had done a lot of reading of articles and books on "cordel" and northeastern folklore at the Institute in 1966 and consulted their fine collection of broadsides of "cordel, and in the process had met many of their researchers, the "cream of the crop" in Northeastern Brazil – Mário Souto Maior, Mauro Mota, Roberto Mota, Sylvio Rabelo and especially Renato Carneiro Campos who had a monograph on "Cordel," perhaps the first in Brazil. So I went first to the last gentleman, offered the manuscript in Portuguese for him to read and was instructed to come back in a day or two and we would talk. So far, so good. I only learned later that plagiarism and downright stealing of manuscripts was rampant. Ah, the naïve gringo!

Senhor Carneiro Campos did read the perhaps 125 - page manuscript, waxed enthusiastic and declared parts of it would be perfect for the Journal of the Institute. So, he, a chauffeur, and I drove to the estate of no less than Gilberto Freyre of "The Masters and the Slaves" fame and founder of the IJNPS on an old sugar cane plantation owned by the family. (I had fallen asleep in one of Freyre's monotoned lectures back in 1966, a mortal sin in those parts.) It's crazy; I remember the drive, the car being parked, but think I was told to stay in the car and the good professor would deal with his boss. I'm sure I never met His Eminence. More good fortune! Mr. Freyre enthusiastically agreed to publish part of the dissertation in an article in the prestigious research review of the Institute.

So, one thinks "Terrific!" My first published article! (Two important ones will come in the "Revista Brasileira de Folclore" of the "Campanha Nacional de Folclore" in Rio, but not treated here.) Well, uh, no. I had bigger aspirations, bigger fish to fry! I wanted the dissertation, if possible, to be published in its entirety as a small book. So, I thanked Mr. Carneiro Campos, probably spoke flattering words of Gilberto Freyre, thanked them all, etc. and said I would think about it. The "bigger fish" was not really a bigger fish, just a different big one – my first mentor for the Ph.D. research in Recife – Ariano Suassuna. I met Ariano at his office near the Law School in June of 1969, now as Cultural Director of the State of Pernambuco. He was dealing with a Peruvian who was producing "Auto da Compadecida" in Lima but based on a translation of the play third hand – Portuguese to French to English to Spanish! Suassuna just laughed.

I showed Ariano the manuscript; he read it the next few days and declared that the University of Pernambuco should publish the whole thing as a small book! He himself would do the "corrections" from my Portuguese. Once again, the University automobile with the chauffeur to the Press, Ariano shows the manuscript, the Director of the Press says "Sim, senhor." And Ariano says it is a done deal. This is June; should be out in August! I am almost not believing what I am hearing. It was all so fortuitous. Suassuna was the "icon" of Northeastern culture in those days, a real "manda-chuva" ["rainmaker"] or "bamba do bairro" [shaker and mover].

One problem: from three months to four years passed before I received the package of 20 copies of the published book in the mail at ASU. It was instrumental in garnering the promotion to Associate Professor with tenure in 1973. (Along with those two research articles in the journal of folklore at the prestigious National Campaign of Folklore in Rio de Janeiro with Vicente Salles its chief.)

In retrospect, I sometimes wonder why Suassuna wanted the book. Could it be that one of the chapters dealt with his work, the "Auto da Compadecida," ["The Rogue's Trial"] utilizing three story-poems of Leandro Gomes de Barros as its plot? Or the wonderful written interviews with "cordel" poets? I shall never know. But "Fortuna" (Toole's "A Confederacy of Dunces") smiled on me again. Suassuna or someone at the press arranged for the cover to utilize a woodcut by no less than J. Borges. He began doing his woodcuts and writing some story-poems in 1965 in a tiny town west of Recife, so we were true contemporaries. He is today the master, número uno, of woodcut artists in all Brazil, his prints sometimes selling for thousands of dollars in Europe, the U.S., as well as Brazil. As I have said, sometimes you live right! See the partial cover above; it depicts the "miracle" of the host turning to blood in the mouth of the holy woman Maria de Araújo in a mass celebrated by no less than Padre Cícero, an icon in the religious story-poems of "cordel."

The short book presents an introduction to the "literatura de cordel," an introduction to its most famous poet, Leandro Gomes de Barros, written interviews with several poets from the 1960s, and finally, an essay on how major national erudite writers borrowed from the "cordel" in their works. A small bibliography of the times follows.

Off to the races you say? Number two will be eight years down the road. But participation in a major book on Brazil on "Cordel" that would help boost me up the academic ladder did come out that same year of 1973, and it's a good story.

Estudos. Literatura Popular em Verso

I think it was in the Spring of 1973 because I was in the office at work. An air mail – special delivery letter came from Varig Airlines Office in Los Angeles informing me they had a round trip ticket from Los Angeles to Rio de Janeiro waiting for me, sometime in early June. No details why. I called them, getting permission for a long-distance call from the always belt – tightening Department of Foreign Languages, and they said it was from an Ana Maria Barroso from the Casa de Rui Barbosa in Rio de Janeiro. I tell all about this in another book. I went to Rio, attended a high falutin' "Primeiro Congresso Internacional de Filologia Portuguesa e 'Os Lusíadas' de Luís de Camões." There was a session on "cordel," and at the young academic age of 32 I was involved with the cream of the crop professors and writers from Portugal, Germany, Italy, and of course, Brazil. All went well and it was an adventure, hilarious at times.

Just one part of the festivities was a special night and party in the "Salão Nobre" [Ballroom] of the Casa de Rui Barbosa in Botafogo. There was food and drink aplenty, great samba music and dancing, but also an intellectual event: the book party for the publishing of "Literatura Popular em Verso. Estudos I." (Another in the seminal series of "Cordel" in all Brazil in the 1960s.) The Casa was instrumental in "saving" or "rescuing" the remnants of old "cordel" in the Northeast and putting the thousands of story-poems in cardboard alphabetized boxes in the old "Research Center Annex" of the Casa. Researchers were welcome, and eventually anyone who was anyone made that trek to Botafogo. That little, cramped Annex is where I sat for hours on end, day after day, week after week in 1967 reading hundreds of story-poems by Leandro Gomes de Barros and other pioneer "cordel" poets, taking notes on 3 X 5 note cards. These would be the basis for a good part of the Ph.D. dissertation. I returned in 1969 for more of the same. There was one moment when the Director of the Research Center Professor Thiers Martins Moreira came into the tiny reading area, called me over and simply said "Tome Nota" ["Take notes."]. A true Brazilian Professor! He proceeded to tell me the whole story of S.E.M.T.A. the organization for providing workers from the Northeast during the Rubber Boom days in the Amazon, reported in "cordel" by a worker or two who also wrote "cordel."

In sum, he must have thought enough of my work to invite me four years later, a relative youngster, to participate in the above book. It is the company you keep! I wrote a long article or chapter taken from the best of the dissertation on the poet Leandro Gomes de Barros and his forté of satiric narrative poetry. The book would be important when it would come time for application for tenure and promotion. The participants tell the whole story: Manuel Diégues Júnior with the main long introduction, really a medium sized book, Ariano Suassuna, Braúlio do Nascimento, Dulce Martins Lamas, Raquel de Queiróz, Sebastião Nunes Batista and yours truly. They all at that time were the "luminaries" of "cordel" research, Brazilian Folklore and icons of Northeastern Literature! Living right!

2

Jorge Amado e a Literatura de Cordel. Salvador: Fundação Cultural do
Estado da Bahia – Fundação Casa de Rui Barbosa, 1981. 95 pp.

Jorge Amado e a Literatura de Cordel

This book is an interesting story, although a bit long. Here we go. On a sabbatical leave from ASU in 1975 I wrote this book from my trailer "office" parked next to the house on Palmcroft Drive in Tempe, AZ. It did not take too long, perhaps two months, this before traveling with wife Keah to Colombia to investigate the Spanish Colonial Heritage (see the report on that in a future book from Trafford.)

The book is small, perhaps a "large monograph," and had as its subject the use of novelist Jorge Amado of anything from "Cordel." Background was from a Brazilian Literature course at Saint Louis University by Professor Doris Turner and her dissertation on his early works. I added three recent novels, "Pastores da Noitc, "Tcnda dos Milagres," and most important, "Teresa Batista Cansada de Guerra" where Amado uses "cordel" format and story-poems in the entire book. I add the disclaimer that my book treated just a small slice of Amado's huge narrative output over the years. I sent the manuscript to the Fundação Casa de Rui Barbosa in Rio where I had done years of research. No less then Adriano Kury Philologist and Director of the Philology Sector which housed the "cordel" library corrected the Portuguese. Adriano was also the most successful mentor for aspiring upper class Brazilians preparing to take the Portuguese Language Exam for entry into the Brazilian State Department (Itamarati). But as usual there were no funds to publish the book so it remained "na gaveta" [in the desk drawer].

Jump forward a few years to 1981 in Salvador, Bahia where they were getting ready for a huge shindig: "50 Anos de Literatura de Jorge Amado" sponsored by the Fundação Cultural do Estado da Bahia. Edilene Matos and Carlos Cunha were organizing it all – a huge celebration in the Mercado Modelo. There would be national press coverage and TV and Nobel Prize winner Vargas Llosa from Peru (a good friend of Amado) representing television from Peru.

"Fortuna" once again! Edilene was searching for a book to publish related to the event and perusing titles from the FCRB, discovered my now dusty manuscript. They worked out a way to co-edit the book, invited me to come to Salvador for the book party, and it turned into up to that time my best moment in publishing in Brazil. I've told the whole story in another book – interviews by "Isto É" the national news magazine, invited by Jorge Amado to his home, the big celebration itself (Bahia knows how to give a party) with national TV news coverage, and finally the book signing party at the newest bookstore in a new shopping center. Amado, Zélia his wife, the national reporters and TV were there to document it all. I include one photo from that wonderful moment:

Mark Curran and Jorge Amado

Proud as a peacock, huh? And even better, the cover was done by no less than Calasans Neto, one of the major illustrators of all of Amado's novels. And even better again was a celebratory dinner of Bahian food (uh oh) at the Mercado Modelo hosted by Jorge Amado where I sat next to him and Zélia with Vargas Llosa and wife Patricia across the table. There would be other fine moments in Brazil in years to come, but this still tops them all!

Vargas Llosa, Jorge and Zélia Amado

The book along with more articles would garner a promotion to Full Professor at ASU in perhaps 1983. Dear reader, it does not get any better than this! And it did not, that is, for a long time.

3

A Presença de Rodolfo Coelho Cavalcante na Moderna Literatura de Cordel. Rio de Janeiro: Editora Nova Fronteira – Fundação Casa de Rui Barbosa, 1987. 324 pp.

A Presença de Rodolfo Coelho Cavalcante na Moderna Literatura de Cordel

In the 1980s in terms of research and writing I moved on to a new phase: "cordel" in Bahia. Earlier reading and work have pointed toward the topic: two poets, one-time competitors, and rivals on the opposite sides of the coin - the iconoclastic Cuíca de Santo Amaro whom I dubbed "the folk-popular hell's mouth of Bahia" and the archconservative, self-proclaimed leader of "cordel" as well as self-promotion of his own works, Rodolfo Coelho Cavalcante.

I was working assiduously on a study on Rodolfo Coelho Cavalcante. In short, RCC claimed to have written and edited (or paid for printing) the amazing total of 1,700 story-poems of "cordel" dating from the early 1940s in Piaui State, then almost 40 years in Salvador, Bahia where he made his home and center of activity. Rodolfo did not have the gift of writing the "romances" of "cordel," but he did have the gift of verse and wrote endlessly in 8-page broadsides mainly of moral and religious themes, politics and current events, and his specialty – biography of dozens of local and national figures.[1] He was extremely proud that "At least 50 per cent of my books have a moral message. A good message." The one he says sold at least, are you ready, one-half million copies was "A Moça que Bateu na Mãe na Sexta-Feira da Paixão e Virou Cachorro" ["The Girl Who Beat Up Her Mother on Good Friday and Was Turned into a Dog"].

Equally important, Rodolfo was a promotor in his time, first of his own work though self-printed and self-paid journals or magazines, but then his self-proclaimed role as "leader of the poetic class." He truly did both. It is a long story, but suffice to say, Rodolfo was responsible for making "cordel" known to the rest of Brazil, especially in the south in Rio de Janeiro and São Paulo. He organized national congresses of the poets and poet-singers in 1955 in Salvador and 1960 in São Paulo. My study was in two parts: his biography and accomplishments and a select anthology of his story-poems. An incidental reward is that in his journals and thousands of letters he chronicled "cordel" as no one else from the 1950s to his death in 1986.

We were in touch during the early research in Brazil in 1966. I intended to meet him then and investigate all this. He was ensconced in a truly modest house in Jequié in the interior of

---

[1] Rodolfo would pick the person, write the story-poem, print a thousand copies and then expect a "gift" or "donation" from the person. He was immensely successful in this endeavor and it kept him going for years.

Bahia and we never met. But he wrote one of the best written interviews via the mail for the 1973 Pernambuco book and we corresponded until I would meet him, do extensive interviews, and collect hundreds of his story-poems in Salvador in that same summer of 1981.

In the next four years I got nowhere with the effort to publish the book and in fact was despondent about even continuing research on Brazil or "cordel." I won't go into the efforts in Salvador, none brought to fruition and truly disheartening. But Lady Fortune smiled once again from an unexpected source, the short story writer and early "aficionado" of "cordel" from the 1950s in Rio de Janeiro, Orígenes Lessa. He was instrumental along with Manuel Diégues Júnior and Manuel Cavalcanti Proença for the FCRB's collection of "cordel." I had begun to read and take copious notes of story-poems in his wonderful library in his apartment in Rio.

When I shared my lack of luck and stonewalling in Salvador he came up with an idea: take the RCC manuscript to no less than Nova Fronteira, then perhaps one of the top commercial publishers in Brazil, incidentally where his books were successful. So, we got on a bus, went to the main offices, and met Sérgio Lacerda, the head of the company (one of the sons of famous "muckraker" Carlos Lacerda who really brought the end of the Getúlio Vargas era). Orígenes graciously "pushed" my book and offered co-publishing with the money from the poor FCRB where he now ramrodded the "Cordel" center.

Lacerda was skeptical, saying NF did not do the type of book of RCC, but agreed to go ahead. This was approximately in 1985. The book came out in 1986, but there was no budget for advertising or promotion. I hauled a whole box of copies home to Tempe but learned later that perhaps 200 copies were gathering dust and mold in the basement "porão" at the Casa. They never did leave the place and it was and still is the worst case of distribution of any of my books in Brazil!

Oh well. The RCC book represents solid research and writing and as mentioned, really told the story not only of Rodolfo but all the "cordel" in his time.

There however was another moment in those days. Orígenes told of a competition sponsored by the FCRB and his own "Biblioteca Orígenes Lessa" in the small, but out of the way city of

Lençois Paulista, São Paulo State, for a monograph on "Cordel." The prize would be called "The Sebastião Nunes Batista Prize" honoring the longtime wonderful researcher at the FCRB and incidentally a good friend. Orígenes encouraged me to send in an entry. Once again, the ole' professor had one in the "gaveta," "A Literatura de Cordel e 'Grande Sertão: Veredas," that long article I wrote in a cabin on Grand Mesa in Colorado probably in 1972. I'll speak more of it later in this narrative, suffice to say, I won the competition (learning only much later there were forty entries from major writers and professors in Brazil and elsewhere). It garnered me and wife Keah a trip to Brazil later that year in 1985, a "second honeymoon," a scary car ride from São Paulo out to Lençois, local speeches at the small library, and incidentally getting to see two major sugar cane refineries (Sugar cane is the major crop in all that part of Brazil). One was a small, old-fashioned "bangüê" [mill] like the ones seen earlier on the José Lins do Rego plantations in Paraíba in 1966, but the other was a modern, huge refinery, an example of the best in Brazil then. I tell it all in another book, suffice to say we traveled on the old Varig Air Pass and had wonderful times in Rio, Salvador and the Hotel Rio Negro in Manaus. Orígenes always thought my down-to-earth, jargon free writing on "cordel" was just the ticket!

After the trip an old nemesis surfaced: no money 'mon' either in Lençois or at the Casa in Rio to print that manuscript. There were months and even years of promises for publication, but nothing came of it. Felicitous, because it had a better ending later at Brown University in Providence, another tale to be told later in this narrative.

But it was in those days, and later after his untimely death, Origenes's wife Maria Eduarda Lessa allowed me to read, take notes and then xerox story-poems from his second to none "cordel" collection on the topic of Brazilian History and Politics that would be instrumental for my most successful book in Brazil, but that's a story to be told later.

4

Cuíca de Santo Amaro Poeta – Repórter da Bahia.
Salvador: Fundação Casa de Jorge Amado, 1990.197 pp.

cuíca
de santo amaro
poeta - repórter
da bahia

Cuíca de Santo Amaro. Poeta – Repórter da Bahia

Cuíca was a scurrilous sort who in effect chronicled in his story-poems all the local and some of the national and international events for about 25 years! He wrote of scandal in the city, extorted money from subjects he bribed to NOT publish the story-poems on them, landed in jail a few times, but truly chronicled local, state and national politics in the Getúlio Vargas era. I had begun readings of Cuíca's story-poems as early as 1978 on a perhaps three-month research endeavor in Rio de Janeiro at the library of the Fundação Casa de Rui Barbosa. I had learned of him from Jorge Amado's guidebook to Salvador ("Bahia de Todos os Santos") and Dias Gomes's famous play made movie "Pagador de Promessas." After a first reading of the extant story-poems at the FCRB, I returned home and wrote the first draft of a possible book. In a major research return to Brazil in 1981 (in June and July, prior to the Amado event in November), I was now in constant contact with my "cicerones" [guide-hosts] Carlos Cunha and Edilene Matos. I showed Carlos the initial draft of the manuscript; he waxed enthusiastic and shared newspaper clippings about Cuíca with me and took me to meet Cuíca's widow in the proletarian sector of Liberdade in Bahia. He also showed me Cuíca's "poor-man's" grave, "cova de rasa." I returned home, wrote a more complete version of the book, sent it to Edilene Matos at the Fundação Cultural do Estado da Bahia where it once again ended in the "gaveta." What Carlos and Edilene did *not* tell me was that she was preparing her own book on Cuíca! Hmm. It would turn out all right.

Time has passed, details are fuzzy, but THIS was the period of no luck in getting anything published in Brazil, either on Cuíca or Rodolfo. That time and aspect of Brazil is something I would rather not repeat, at least in any detail. I have never begged or bought publication in Brazil but learned indirectly from Carlos Cunha that most books in Brazil are paid for by the author himself! Time passed and then Carlos said one fine day, "Why don't you write to Jorge Amado himself and see what he says?" Friends, my six-gun had only one more bullet. I'll never know for sure why Amado did what he did, but it was his "Bahia de Todos os Santos" when he wrote of Cuíca in 1944 that had initiated my interest in it all, and Jorge had followed Cuíca's entire career. Long story made short: he not only arranged for his own foundation in Salvador, "Fundação Casa de Jorge Amado," to publish the book but he would write the preface-presentation himself! Meu Deus! Living right again and Lady Fortuna smiling down. That was a one-time deal!

The book highlights the literary, historical scene in Salvador during Cuíca's days in the 1940s to his death in 1964, views of him by those who knew him, both admirers and enemies,[2] his own self-portrait in verse, his own choice of role as poet-reporter of Bahia, and an anthology of many story-poems.

I probably sent the final manuscript in the late 1980s and it came out in 1990, now the fourth book in Brazil. The story of all this is interesting and a bit unbelievable! I'm not sure but believe the Jorge Amado Foundation was only begun after that memorable "50 Years of Literatura de Jorge Amado" in 1981. It is in one of the most historic places in Brazil – the Pelourinho Plaza of Salvador. When I arrived and saw it for the first time, what a thrill! It is in one of the 400-year-old "sobrados" of perhaps four stories, of course, remodeled, painted in vivid colors and really a classy place (I think in the same time frame as when the municipality really fixed up the entire plaza, badly in need of a makeover from my early years there in 1966). It serves as the repository of everything of Jorge Amado and secondarily as a bookstore for all his works, and a venue for lectures, concerts and in my case: the publication autograph party.

Once again, I tell the whole story in another book, so will just hit the highlights here. Carlos Cunha did the publicity and Myriam Fraga the Foundation director took care of the details. The book is just one of the series "Casa de Palavras" and I am told I was indeed in good company with the many fine books in the series. The fly-leaf photo of yours truly was taken from the hot fourth story window with the historic churches in the background. I can't remember all the details of the party but there were "caipirinhas" of the local fruits, "comes e bebes" [eats and drinks], the attendance of the local literary luminaries of the times, television and newspaper reporters. The format was a few speeches in the customary "Bahian baroque" style and then a "debate" where I was to defend my book and its contents. That went well, but I don't remember the details. The crowd was small, probably the most exciting moment the ravings of iconoclastic "cordel" poet

---

[2] The reader has to put up with a personal observation. I fantasized the scene and moment from a reading of one of my favorite Jorge Amado Novels, "Tenda dos Milagres," ["The Miracle Shop"] in which Amado expertly portrays the acerbic, back-biting, literary scene of the times and the battle for his hero Pedro de Arcanjo and Afro-Brazilian culture to be recognized in Salvador. There is a minor figure, a north American writer and professor who comes to Bahia, discovers Pedro and writes a book about the whole thing. And indirectly influences the prejudiced locals to accept Pedro.

Lucena de Mossoró, but with the presence of Cuíca's illustrator Sinésio Alves and Cuica's widow. (Cunha assured me that a nice monetary present was given to her that evening.) Cunha later attributed the relatively small crowd to peoples' fear of going to the Pelourinho at night! Hmm.

Sinésio's work and contribution at the book party follow:

Sinésio Alves and Cardboard Cuíca Mockup

It was a short visit to Brazil, perhaps one week, so a day or two later I traipsed up to the Foundation, went to the second floor and asked for copies of my book. I was assured they would all be duly mailed to me, but I insisted on taking at least part, perhaps ten to 20 copies with me then. A good thing: the large part promised was never sent or at least never arrived at ASU. Cunha told me later the book sold out immediately, not because of me necessarily, but because Cuíca was such a memorable memory in the city. Me, I'm most proud of that complimentary "apresentação" by Jorge Amado. I learned he does many of them, his "imprimatur" a prize for any aspiring writer in Salvador.

In sum, the moment did not come close to the "50 Years" falderal in 1981, but who is to complain?

5

La Literatura de Cordel Brasileña: Antología Bilingüe. La
Lira de Licario. Madrid, Orígenes, 1991. 211 pp.

A publishing hiatus in Brazil, but not in Spain! This is my only book in Spanish but another
good story.

La Literatura de Cordel Brasileña - Antología Bilingüe.

Ah, Lady Fortuna! While teaching in Professor Michael Flys's ASU Summer School in Spain in 1989, I just by chance met one of his friends and colleagues in Spain, the owner and director of Orígenes Publishing House. This in no way was my doing; it might have been a party or "tertulia." I do not even today have a record of his name, but when this gentleman discovered my interest and extensive publishing on Brazil's "Literatura de Cordel," he grew excited and enthusiastic. He was knowledgeable of the popular literature tradition in Spain (the "romances," the ballads, their own "literatura de cordel" or "literatura de los ciegos) and in Spanish America. But he had only really heard of the same tradition in Brazil. Seeing my work, I'm not sure of the p's and q's, but he immediately requested me to write a bilingual anthology – Portuguese and Spanish – to be published at Orígenes in Madrid.

The book was a real pleasure to do, and the work was done in one academic year, largely in the office at Arizona State U. It would have a short introduction to the phenomenon and history of "cordel" in Brazil and relating it a bit to the same but different Spanish phenomena ("a piece of cake," already done and polished in articles, etc.) a selection of fourteen story-poems reflecting an overview of the themes and best-known works ("another piece of cake," choosing them from research experience, pulling the broadsides down from the shelves in my office), and the main task, translating them to Spanish. Aha!

I was formed in the Ph.D. program of Spanish and Latin American Studies with a minor in Portuguese and Luso- Brazilian Studies, knew well both languages, and in this case had extensive on-site work in Brazil, and mainly – could keep them separate! Double that exclamation point!! One must have the talent, I daresay, and the gift of language, and mainly the desire to do this. Books could be written of the precipices and ravines between Hispanic and Luso-Brazilian cultures and their respective languages. Each says the other is "easy" to learn, but in most cases I have met, there was not much proof of that. I think being a native speaker of English plus that study background did thc trick.

So, in that short one year's time I did the translation. End of bragging rights! I wangled a few hundred dollars to pay one of our Ph.D. students from Spain, Salvador Oropesa, to go over the Spanish translation and as Pedro Salinas the 20th century eminent poet would say, get "la palabra exacta!" We had very enjoyable sessions in my office reviewing the manuscript. One note: Salvador had never been to Brazil, did not know Portuguese, so often I had to "set the scene" for some of the story-poems and their events. But then he quickly and efficiently would know if a similar scene or event could/would be possible in Spain. Truly, humbly, there were relatively few times when the Spanish I generated was not "spot on," but there were enough that proved his participation wonderful in doing a good, correct book.

The problem came when the people at Orígenes came to taking the typed manuscript to press. The draft they sent me was a mess! Our original was not. I can only surmise that the typist or typesetter did not know Portuguese and his/her Spanish confused the two! The Spanish side of the page was fine. It was the Portuguese that was embarrassing. At any rate, after two long sets of reading and sending the corrections, they got most of it right. "Good enough for government work" you might say. It is a fine book and there are not many like it. "Portunhol" you say!

A final note: it would be this experience recalled during retirement when I decided to do a similar thing, but bilingual in English and Portuguese for Trafford Publishing in Bloomington, Indiana. That story is to come.

6

Cuíca de Santo Amaro – Controvérsia no Cordel. São Paulo: Hedra, 2000. 131 pp.

Cuíca de Santo Amaro. Hedra

This very small book was done by request from the long-time "cordel" researcher Joseph Luyten in São Paulo. Luyten had a significant achievement: he convinced Hedra Publishers to do a series of small books on the major writers of "cordel," plus he signed up contemporary researchers to write them. He asked me to do the one on Cuíca, probably because of the success of the original book in Salvador in 1990. It was an easy task because all the research was already one. I did an introductory chapter telling of the highlights of Cuíca and then picked twelve story-poems for the anthology. One of them is his famous and true poem of the woman who grew tired of her unfaithful and drunken husband, and when he passed out in bed after a night of carousing, she, uh, well, cut it off! (A similar event happened in the United States – the Bobbit affair.)

I also included three of his stories on national and international politics and two or three that symbolized his views on the deceit, scandal and more in Bahian politics and life.

I would rather have done the volume on João Martins de Atayde or Leandro Gomes de Barros, better poets than Cuíca, but oh well.

7

História do Brasil em Cordel. Editora da Universidade de São Paulo: São Paulo, 1998. 288 pp.

História do Brasil em Cordel

This book with several printings was the most successful commercially of all my academic books in Brazil, do doubt due to its publisher: the University Press of the University of São Paulo, the most prestigious of such presses in Brazil. May I repeat the cliché? Lady Fortuna! I should get off that, or at least add, that all was the result of very hard work and persistent work over fifty years. That is more accurate. But Lady Luck and who knows the luck of the Irish played a role. This book has a very interesting genesis and story.

From the very beginning in 1966 I came to realize the journalistic function of part of "cordel," and in fact the first or second article was titled "History and Politics in Brazil's 'Literatura de Cordel, '"an unassuming, small monograph by the Latin American Center at ASU, read by no one, but hey it still counted. Whoops, got off the subject there. Trying to keep it simple, you can boil down the functions of "cordel" to 1 Entertain 2 Inform 3 Teach, probably in that order. The vast majority of the more than 100,000 titles are meant to entertain. Perhaps five to ten percent deal with current events, politics, or history. But just the same and the poets always said this, "We are the main source of news for our humble readers." You could put it another way, and I did in writings: "Cordel" was and is the newspaper of the poor humble class and the poets its "reporters."

One writer, critic and poet criticized me heavily for this, paraphrasing, Curran thinks "cordel" is only journalism. He obviously had not read "Retrato do Brasil em Cordel," to come. Or any of the academic journal articles for that matter.

Yet, what can I say? "História do Brasil em Cordel" sold thousands of copies and I did reap some economic benefit, the only time in 50 years. Once again, one reason: the University of São Paulo, its prestigious press, and a truly efficient distribution system.

The genesis: happenstance? Lady Fortuna? Or being in the right place at the right time. Or just living right.

I can't recall how I heard of it, but Brown University in Providence was having a conference on Portugal and Brazil and respective cultures. Oh, maybe it was Professor Thomas Skidmore who informed me. It would be the Fall of 1994. I thought, hey I do one conference per year, and this should be the one: New England for the first time, Fall in New England, meeting the crowd at prestigious Brown (known for being n. 1 in Portuguese Language and Culture of Portugal in the U.S.), a major professor linked to my work teaching there, Thomas Skidmore, and what else? Oh, it turned out the New England Portuguese food was terrific, and I got to walk all through Newport in fall foliage after the meeting.

That wasn't the most important, as we shall see.

Due to past research, collecting and writing I had a wonderful batch of the "cordel" stories that talked of politics and history, and many of them were full of humor and satire. So I put a paper together and got on the plane to Providence.

I was lodged in very comfortable "guest" housing and had time to wander all about campus, totally different from the new and shiny "western" look of ASU, Brown was, as they say, "old money." Most buildings of dark brick, and yes, lots of ivy (Brown is Little Ivy league). And the Rhode Island School of Art and Design (I hope that's the right name) is next door. I can't remember the order of things, but I sat in on classes by the renowned Professor Skidmore and a second person, Brown's top professor of Brazilian studies and language. I recall the classrooms seemed be more like living rooms; aside from desks, tables and chairs, there were easy chairs, divans and even fireplaces! Wow, I thought; I could get used to this.

So, the day of the conference and talks arrived. I have no recall of the title of the session, but all was arranged (it was a small conference) so that all the participants could attend each session and talks. My talk on politics and history in the "cordel" was full of humor and much laughter by all (credit the poets, huh?). Afterward, a fellow came up, said he loved the talk, that it really was "spot on" for talking about Brazil. Then he introduced himself: Sérgio Miceli, President (like CEO) of the University Press of the University Press of São Paulo. "I want this to be known in Brazil! Write up the whole thing and send it to me soon!"

I don't think he was used to anyone saying no, ever, and believe me I didn't! I probably stammered a thank you and yes as soon as it is ready!

Curran, are you still living right?

The next two years I finished what would be "História do Brasil em Cordel," careful to say that "cordel" was not history or even popular history, but that it was and is an excellent source for those who write history. The book would cover "cordel's" treatment of major national events beginning with the War of Canudos in 1896, the "Turbulent Years" of 1920 to 1930, The Age of Getúlio Vargas from 1930 to 1964, The Return to Democracy from 1955 to 1964, "Brazil – love it or leave it – synthesis of an age," 1964 to 1985, and finally, from 1985 to the Present, "After the Euphoria, a Return to the Normal." I would first tell of the historical moment then give "cordel's'" take on it, liberally quoting from the story-poems. Anytime I needed help, I quoted either E. Bradford Burns (major U.S. Historian on Brazil) or Thomas Skidmore (the same in History and Politics). It turns out to be a fine study.

The best is yet to come. By 1996 I had mailed the manuscript to Brazil and figured out a way to get there, reading a paper at a conference at USP. The academic conference was the lesser part; what really counted was going to the offices of the press on campus, meeting the fellow who oversaw preparing my book, the arrival of Sérgio himself, all smiles, "Did you forget your Portuguese? Ha ha." Echoing Ariano Suassuna in 1969 he said it's all set, all we need is a title, how about "História do Brasil em Cordel?" Okay. Done deal. He added, come by next Tuesday and we'll sign the contracts."

Curran has arrived at the gates of a professor's heaven! An aside, I brought with me perhaps 100 story-poems of "cordel" that matched the topics and illustrated them with either photo-clichés or woodcuts. Sérgio loved them as did the publishing team and amazingly enough included ALL OF THEM in the final book, plus a "photo gallery of the poets" in color at the end. People, this was starting to be a fine, fine book. Oh, incidentally, that was in large part due to Plínio Martins, Chief of Publishing at the press. He will enter my story much more soon, suffice to say, a very felicitous moment.

In sum, the book came out in 1998 with a large printing (for academic books) followed by two more in 2000 and 2001. And amazing enough, there were very significant payments of author's rights. The book really became an academic success largely, as said, because of the wonderful USP bookstore and distribution system. It does not hurt to be in a city of 20 million and be the best university in the country.

In a commercial sense, it's all downhill from there, but $$ were never the motive. USP and "História" were the publishing heights of a long career from 1969 to retirement in 2002.

There is a happy addendum: due to this contact with Brown and their knowledge of my work, I was invited to submit an article to their prestigious journal. Aha! The reader may recall "Grande Sertão: Veredas e a Literatura de Cordel," the Sebastião Nunes Batista Prize in 1985, the subsequent lack of funding and the study in the "gaveta" [desk drawer] at the FCRB. Well, it now would become the lead article in "Brasil/ Brazil" N. 14, Ano 8, 1995. I did a comparison of texts between the novel and the broadsides of the heroic cycle of cordel; the thesis being that both shared an astounding "substratum" of topics or themes. Recall it was this study that won that contest in Brazil and a trip for wife Keah and me in 1985. I think it might have ruffled the feathers of many "professores tradicionais" in Linguistics and Literary Theory.

Brasil/ Brazil

8

Retrato do Brasil em Cordel. São Paulo: Ateliê, 2011. 365 pp.

Retrato do Brasil em Cordel

This book is the highlight and best of the academic books done before retirement and has a story to tell. Knowing I was edging toward retirement yet in the late 1990s, I began perusing the entire "cordel" collection then housed on the shelves of my office at ASU. Previous work had been leading me to the notion of this book: "Cordel" in all its immensity in the 20th century truly does present a portrait of Brazil and somehow, I wanted to tell that story. Hmm you say. Not easy. The sum is the total of its parts, so I began to organize the collection of perhaps three thousand story-poems into the themes or "cycles" I always believed they represented. "Cordel" seemed to me to be a true folk-popular epic so the structure would follow the classic European epic of 10 chapters (they used "cantos"). It is worthwhile to summarize them here:

1. God Above and Below: in This We Believe
   (Jesus, Mary, the Saints, The Devil and all his mischief)

2. The Manifestations
   (Sebastianism, Messianic Figures and Popular Catholicism

   – Antônio Conselheiro, Padre Cícero, Frei Damião)

   (Catholics, Protestants and Cachaça, Brazilian Spiritism, the Pope, and Rome)

3. What One Should Not Do: The Recompense of Sin
   (Sin and the Moral State of the World/ Woman, a modern Eve / From the Cabaré to the Prostitute/ Horns/ Modern Making Out/ On the Beach/ The Things They Wear!/ Hippies, drugs and Rock n' Roll)

   (The Moral Example/ the Phenomena)

4. A Model for Life: The Heroes of "Cordel"
   (Carlos Magno/ European Fairy Tales and a Magic Peacock/ The Animal Hero/ The Anti-Hero)

   (Real life heroes: the bandits and brave back landers)

5. Life Is a Struggle: Life Is an Odyssey
   (Difficult times in the days of Leandro Gomes de Barros)

   (The Droughts and the consequences: migration to the South)

6. We Have Our Distractions
   (The "cantador" and the "cantoria")

   ("Cordel as diversion – the poet and the market)

   ("Funny" stories)

   ("Futbol")

7. In Politics We Believe but Do Not Trust
   (The War of Canudos and the Old Republic/ Getúlio Vargas, "Father of the Poor"/
   Democracy and Chaos from 1954 to 1965/ The Military Government and "Pax Militar"/
   The Return to "normal" in the present)

8. There's A Big World Out There
   (World War I, World War II, International Conflict in the Modern Era/ Satire of and
   from the Third World)

9. Life Is Getting More Difficult
   (The Right to Be Born/ The Right to Be different – the Modern Feminist/ Rights of
   a Husband and Wife/ Rights of Children/ Rights of the Marginalized/ The Case of
   Roberta Close/ Violence and Death on the Streets, the Country and the Planet)

10. This Is Not the End
    (Utopia on Earth – "Viagem a São Saruê"/ Remembering the Brazilians – "Vida e Morte
    de …" / The Arrival in Heaven or Hell/ "All on Earth Will End")

It took 361 published pages in large format, two columns to a page: 722 "normal" pages, but I did it! I retold the story of "Cordel." The title is based upon a famous academic book by Paulo Prado in 1928, a bellwether look at his country in the heady days of Brazilian "Modernismo." In its own way, "Retrato" does the same but based on the story-poems of the humble northeastern poets of the 20th century. I would not have been able to write such a mammoth book withing knowing at least of the possibility of its being published. The reader may recall when USP did "História do Brasil em Cordel" in 1998, that I met Plínio Martins, the set-up man for all EDUSP'S books. Plínio Martins also ran his own press, Ateliê Editorial in São Paulo, really a press for the most esoteric, fine works of writing. Eexamples: a one thousand page compendium of "Os Sertões" ["Rebellion in the Back Lands] or James Joyce's "Ulysses" in Portuguese! The "literatura de cordel" certainly had no place in that rare air! But Plíno was one of the persons who really understood it, its history from the scholars and volumes on "Cordel" at the FCRB in Rio, and the fresh look at Brazilian History in my book at USP. He told me in 1998 when I was at the Press (paraphrasing): I can do a much better book for you than "História," much better and finer. And beautiful! (He was thinking of the woodcuts used to illustrate much of "cordel" since the 1960s). So, banking on that rather vague promise I spent probably two years organizing and writing the book. Sometimes you take chances.

I delivered the manuscript (a first draft to Ateliê but many more to me after much editing and reworking the manuscript before sending it to Plínio in about 2002.) I retired, the years passed, the book was not "in the drawer" ["na gaveta"] as others, but just stalled. Plínio had too many books to do, he told me a list of over 200, so I would have to be patient. Ha! I'm used to that drill in Brazil. But after some time and no proofs to read, I traveled to São Paulo, sat down with his text revisor, a competent young lady from Southern Brazil, and she basically told me it needed a lot of work, and she was only through two or three chapters. What to do?

The young lady was replaced on this project, I'll never know the details: exasperation, other interests, other projects at Ateliê, working and raising a family? I do know she was not enamored of Brazilian folk – popular story-poems. But Plínio still had the vision. A new text editor Geraldo Gerson de Souza came in and after about a year and a half produced an incredibly fine, artful final text of the book, correcting my Portuguese, but not changing the text in the least. I had provided perhaps two hundred photo-clichés and woodcut prints to illustrate the immense book, and Ateliê used them all!

The book also tells of all my travels and ups and downs over fifty years to research and write of "cordel," with mention, interviews or anecdotes of the poets, the printers, and the Brazilian "high" literature writers who used "cordel" as inspiration or in some cases, plagiarized it in their own works! The result was one fine book, in some ways like a fine "coffee table" book for its size and polish. An artist was hired who did a wonderful cover (we could not use the covers of "cordel" themselves due to copyright notions). Fine paper, perfect revision and editing, no typos I ever discovered (720 column pages). But an inevitable result: in 2010 when it finally came out, the price was 75 reais, $35 dollars in Brazil. Astronomical for even the average Brazilian book buyer.

For whatever reason the book was not marketed widely, so sales have never been substantial, nothing at all like "História do Brasil em Cordel" at USP. This is disappointing but not disheartening. Libraries did order it, some good reviews were done, and more importantly, I have it and am proud of it. I, like "cordel," am in rare company at Ateliê, a privilege. More than one reviewer has lamented that it was not "Properly divulged. A pity." I feel no rancor; I did not do it for money. Just an aside, Dr. Chris Dunn Chair of Spanish and Portuguese at Tulane University and President of the national Brazilian Studies Association discovered the book in the Tulane Library and wrote me immediately. One thing led to another and my entire "cordel" library, primary and secondary works, is now housed at the Latin American Library of Tulane. Chris said just the other day, leafing through the pages of "Retrato" when we did a zoom class for his look at the "Cultura do Sertão do Brasil," "A fine book, an amazing book." I'll take that.

PART II

THE RETIREMENT BOOKS

INTRODUCTION TO PART II

The "Retrato" book and the years waiting for its publication in Brazil led to a big decision in retirement. I'm now 62 years old, "Retrato" took about ten years to come to fruition. Hmm. I don't have that much time to wait for the next one. That and another accidental circumstance will lead to big changes in PART II of this book, the 34 volumes published by Trafford Press of Bloomington, Indiana as of March 2023. Self-published yes, regrets, none!

I recall talking to son-in-law Courtney Hinman on a walk at Dobson Ponds, perhaps ten years ago, he asking what I was doing with myself in retirement? Here continues a big part of that story.

Retirement in 2002, a return to music and performance, fishing and hiking, part – time at ASU in the Spring, cultural nights at the Pine River Public Library in Bayfield, Colorado – that was what was happening. Then came a fortuitous evening with friend and intellectual soulmate Richard Arms on Deer Trail Lane at Vallecito Lake in Colorado. Richard a stockbroker in Albuquerque and creator of the Arms Index for the New York Stock Exchange was down deep a literary person steeped in readings of the masters. He also had a bent for creative writing and did a volume on the Chaco Civilization, the Kokopelli figure. It was self-published through Trafford Publishing and Ricard gave me a copy. After reading it, a light went on. Why can't I do this? So, I took baby steps and did the first book.

1

Brazil's Folk Popular Poetry – "A Literatura de Cordel"

A Bilingual Anthology in English and Portuguese

Trafford Publishing, Bloomington, 2010. 159 pp.

Brazil's Folk – Popular Poetry

I rarely if ever check on sales at Trafford, perhaps one time a year, but I think this first book did the best, perhaps because it was adopted in some classrooms. The only "advertising," if you want to call it that, was a blurb on my Facebook Page. And I would add it to the "books" section on my website, www:currancordelconnection.com. [3]

The book was truly fun to do, still basically an "academic" book but without the old process of submitting it to a publisher, waiting weeks or months for the publication committee to decide to publish it or not, then the re-writing, etc. and perhaps publication in a few months. And truly most likely it would be turned down. Academic presses always are short of cash, and publications are few. Now I was in charge. I'll explain the process in depth just for this first Trafford Book.

I did the book because I thought there was a true need for it, I had the knowledge and expertise to do it, and enjoy doing translation. I did an Introduction to Brazil's "Literatura de Cordel" and then translated ten of the story-poems, among them some of the best of the small genre. Before each poem we placed an illustration of its cover and a very short introduction to the poem to place it within the whole of "Cordel." I placed a short bibliography of scholarly books on "Cordel" at the end. We used the covers of six of the poems to illustrate the Trafford cover. Trafford helped the "rookie" with short statements supporting the book on the back cover. And we added a photo of the author, the one used on the Cuíca de Santo Amaro book at the Fundação Jorge Amado in 1990.

It is worthwhile to list the titles of those poems:

1. Debate of the Protestant Preacher with Master Vulture.
    "Debate d'um Ministro Nova-Seita e Urubú"

    Leandro Gomes de Barros

---

[3] Now twelve years and 33 books later, I probably get 200 emails a year and the same in phone calls with people wanting to either share costs with me to publish the same titles, offer incentives for movies, etc. Since I do zero advertising, I don't know how many of the messages are legitimate, but I'm sure a lot are not. Scams, my friends, to make or take some money. I spoke to a person in similar straits who said he decided to "go for it," went on the circuit and sold a bunch of books. By the time he paid for travel, lodging and food he was out a bundle of money. His enthusiasm did not last long. At my age, even if such offers were legit, no need.

2. Money.
   "O Dinheiro"

   Leandro Gomes de Barros

3. The Girl Who Beat Up Her Mother on Good Friday and Was Turned into a Dog.
   "A Moça Que Bateu na Mãe na Sexta-Feira de Paixão e Virou Cachorra"

   Rodolfo Coelho Cavalcante

4. Story of Mariquinha and José de Sousa Leão
   "História de Mariquinha e José de Souza Leão"

   João Ferreira de Lima

5. Sufferings of the Northeasterner Traveling to the South
   "Os Martírios do Nortista Viajando para o Sul"

   Cícero Vieira da Silva, "Mocó"

6. Poetic Duel between Patrick and Ignatius from Catingueira
   "Peleja de Patrício e Inácio da Catingueira"

   Attributed to João Martins de Atayde

7. The Encounter of Tancredo with St. Peter in Heaven
   "O Encontro de Tancredo com São Pedro no Céu"

   Chiquinho do Pandeiro and Mestre Azulão

8. The End of the War and the Death of Hitler and Mussolini
   "O Fim da Guerra e a Morte de HITLER e MUSSOLINE"

   Delarme Monteiro da Silva

9. Debate between Lampão and an American Tourist
   "Debate de Lampião com uma Turista Americana"

   Franklin Maxado Nordestino

10. Trip to São Saruê
    "Viagem a São Saruê"

    Manoel Camilo dos Santos

I suspect the whole thing took less than a year. It appeared on Trafford's website, on Amazon.com and, alas, did not bring fame. I learned there are literally a few million such books published each year. It is an accident if you are discovered. Oh, curious reader, if you want to know more about the book go to Amazon.com, books, put in Mark J. Curran or the title. The defense rests.

2

The Farm. Trafford Publishing, Bloomington, 2010. 189 pp.

MARK J. CURRAN

The FARM

Growing up in Abilene, Kansas, in the 1940s and 1950s

The Farm

More books were to come, not because of any desire to sell them and make money, but because I had something to say and time to fill in retirement. This book, the first of an autobiographic nature has an interesting genesis. Years before retirement, still teaching at Arizona State University, summers were spent generally in two ways: first, teaching summer school, first term ending after July 4th in sweltering Tempe, Arizona, and spending the balance of the summer on our lot near Vallecito Lake in Colorado. Secondly, if I were fortunate enough to get a research grant, it was off to Brazil for a few weeks to get more material for research but also truthfully to enjoy the delights of Brazil. Even then, I would get three or four weeks on our acre.

An aside but apropos: we camped originally in an 8 x10 cotton duck Coleman tent, cooking on a Coleman stove and it was fun. Perhaps five years later we purchased a 23-foot Coachman Travel Trailer and parked it on the acre for the entire summer. If I were going to Brazil, my wife Keah and I would hook up the trailer in Tempe, haul it to Vallecito after school was out in May, and park it for the summer. Keah and later daughter Katie would live in it until I returned.

Now, to the point: in those years of sleeping and living in the trailer, I maintained an "office" in the old Coleman Tent, running an electric line to the tent from the trailer, working on a metal camp table with a Smith-Corona Electric Typewriter plugged into the trailer via a long electric cord. Light (and some heat) were from a Coleman gas lantern hanging from the roof of the 8 X 10 tent. Some of my happiest days were when 3 -year-old Katie would come toddling out to the tent to see me!

Katie at the Office

I am reminded and Keah remembers well. One summer was spent typing for about six hours a day for an entire month to produce the manuscript for that 1987 book in Brazil on the poet Rodolfo Coelho Cavalcante (n. 3 above). Friends used to comment that when driving by our lot on the only road to the mailboxes and highway they would hear the "click, click, click" of that typewriter.

Now, one gets tired of that eventually, and I was tired of academic writing and had a brainstorm to do something of my family, growing up on the farm and school and the rest. I recall I got out a yellow pad and just began to write down memories, one at a time, one line at a time. The memory was in charge, so things were out of order at first, but that was remedied later, chronologically. At that time, I began to type very short vignettes of those days, everything from describing the farm, my parents' history of buying it and living on it, all the memories of growing up, including describing the 100-year-old farmhouse, farm buildings, farm chores, fieldwork, and harvest and much more.

Sometime later, probably now in 2010 I must have typed all those pages on the computer, revised and edited and added the old black and white photos of the 1940s and 1950s. I think because the book was small, I added "school days" from kindergarten to graduation from high school. Dear reader, all this does not happen overnight and not without moments of shall we say, fatigue. But I loved doing it and yet today "The Farm" is one of my favorites. Why? It is memories of all my family, our days and years, economic struggles to keep it all going, and many ups and downs to it all. I can only say that I think there are thousands of farm people that had that same experience and can relate to it.

Fortune was with me for the cover. I do not know the exact fact, but Dickinson County in Kansas was doing a survey of the land and the method was aerial photography of the farms in the country. A perhaps 12 by 12 color photo of the results was presented to each farm owner. Perfect for the book! It shows the northeast corner of the half-section farm in Dickinson County with my favorite part: the pond with all the trees and its history. But crop acreage of plowed land (wheat, alfalfa, or corn) is visible. And finally, the two white strips are the lanes of Interstate 70 which was done during the Eisenhower Administration, perhaps 1958, which took 20 or 30 acres off the north end of the farm via eminent domain. My brother Jim and I would go up and watch the huge earth moving machines, caterpillars, and such during the construction.

The bottom of the front cover is the idea of the clever Trafford designer: old barn wood. And also, on the back cover together with a blurb about the book and the author's picture. So that's it.

The Dickinson County Historical Society asked for some copies, and I have no idea how many sold. Otherwise, the normal, if any, on the Trafford Web Page or Amazon.com 's zillions of books. There were two or three wonderful reviews by I suspect people just like me. Old farmer boys.

3

Coming of Age with the Jesuits. Trafford Publishing, Bloomington, 2012. 151 pp.

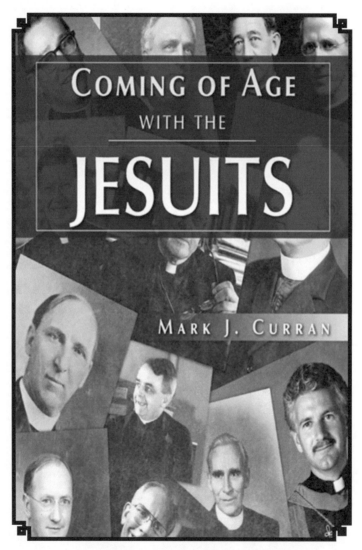

Coming of Age with the Jesuits

One thing led to another. Pleased with "The Farm" and time on my hands, I decided to write up the next few years, meaning the B.S.B.A. at Rockhurst College from 1959 to 1963, including the first experience in Latin America in 1962, and then the study odyssey for the Ph.D. at Saint Louis University from 1963 to 1968. There was an important year spent in Brazil on a Fulbright-Hays Dissertation Research Grant in 1966-1967.

As I wrote in the book, the effort was conversational, in the writing style of a nineteen-year-old off to college from the small farm town and then on to serious graduate work but still finishing at the tender age of twenty-six. Hence the title "Coming of Age with the Jesuits;" it could have been "Growing Up with the Jesuits." An awful lot of water has passed under the bridge regarding my Catholic faith since 1959, but then no real doubts had surfaced, and I was open to the Jesuit educational experience.

No point in going into detail; it's all in the book. Suffice to say my mother wanted her boys to attend Jesuit Schools ("they are good teachers"), and she ought to know, a traditional school-marm in Eastern Colorado and in Central Kansas for years. I went to Rockhurst for all the wrong reasons – major league baseball, the Plaza, the big city – but in the end trusted Mom's views and headed to Kansas City. The four years were interesting, some ups and downs, some surprises, but all according to hoyle. What was different was three months in Mexico City and Guatemala in the summer of 1962 and the experience changed my life! It confirmed the decision to go to graduate school, study Spanish and Latin American Studies, and ended with a career teaching the stuff at Arizona State University from 1968 t0 2011. I'd love to talk about all that, but, hey, it's in the book.

Now accustomed to the Trafford process, it was a breeze: finish the manuscript, get all the photos together in jpeg form, do the Trafford Submission Form, do the proofs as they came, and presto, in rather short time we have the book. Once again, absolutely no regrets going with Trafford. Good quality paper, good printing, a wonderful front and back cover, all I expected.

4

Adventures of a 'Gringo' Researcher in Brazil in the 1960s – In Search of the 'Literatura de Cordel.' Trafford Publishing, Bloomington. 2012. 237 pp.

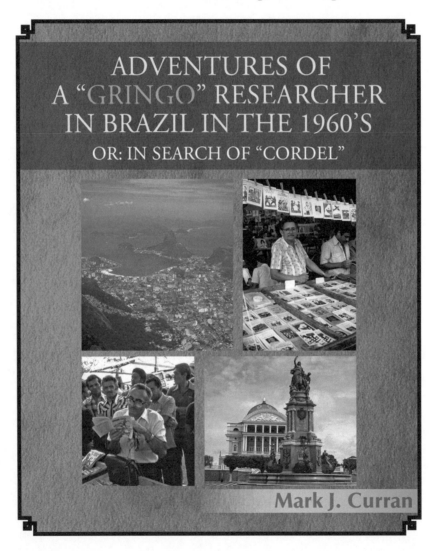

This book would begin an entire series of volumes that would sport on the book covers photos of research and travel from the years at Arizona State University. This volume combined memories of travel and research in Brazil doing the footwork for the Ph.D. dissertation on a Fulbright-Hays research grant in 1966 and 1967. It is solely based on the diary I kept that entire year. This was the eye – opening moment of what would follow for almost fifty years, really a vocation – travel and work in Brazil which produced the volumes in Part I.

It details life, some travail, and a whole lot of fun for Curran the bachelor. Time and a lot of work in Recife, Pernambuco, research jaunts to the northeastern interior to Caruaru, Campina Grande (Paraiba), Juazeiro do Norte (Ceara), Natal (Rio Grande do Norte), Maceió (Alagoas) and then on to Salvador da Bahia. Then four wonderful months in Rio de Janeiro, then once again to the "interior" of Minas Gerais, Brasília the new capital, and an unforgettable trip on a wood burning sternwheeler on the São Francisco River through the back lands of Minas Gerais ad Bahia. Then a final sojourn in Recife and a trip to the Amazon seeing Belém and Manaus. Whew!

I did the research on "cordel," met the poets in the markets, met famous Brazilian intellectuals and spent months reading in research libraries. But I really got to know Brazil, spent too much time on sun drenched beaches, met two or three fine Brazilian young ladies, got to know Brazil's Afro-Brazilian religions, "did" carnival in Rio, and made some good friends. It's all in the book, a good read providing you want to know about the "old days" in better times in Brazil.

The book was written, now with the normal "drill" at Trafford. With a curious aside: it was this book that the personnel person for Lindblad Expeditions – National Geographic happened to see, read, like, and invited me to lecture on the National Geographic Explorer ship on three occasions in later years. Some books were sold to the guests on the ship, and I doubt any more. That story is coming up.

5

Peripécias de um Gringo Pesquisador no Brasil nos Anos 1960
ou à Cata do Cordel. Trafford, 2012, 227 pp.

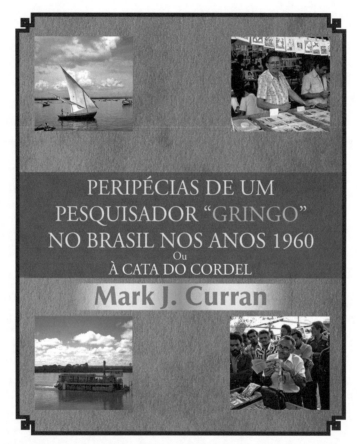

Peripécias de um Pesquisador "Gringo" no Brasil nos Anos 1960

This is the Portuguese version of "Adventures," already seen. The translation is a major effort and really like doing an entirely new book. The motive: make it available for Portuguese language readers.

6

A Trip to Colombia. Highlights of Its Spanish Colonial Heritage. Trafford. Bloomington, 2013. 159 pp.

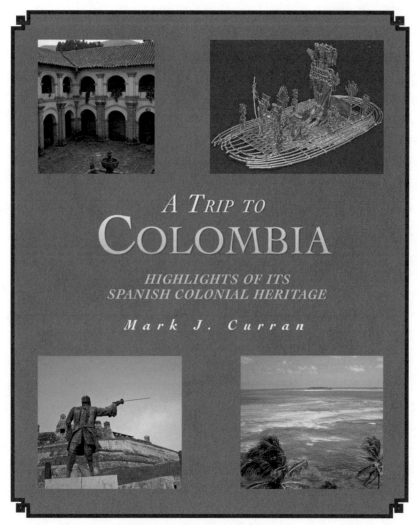

A Trip to Colombia

This book was a delight to do. It is based on the diary of a sabbatical trip to Colombia in the Spring of 1975. The genesis is interesting, and the book will be in the series "Stories I Told My Students." I was in 1974 now teaching the upper division course SPA 472 Spanish American Civilization at ASU, and one of my fine students modestly suggested there was something I was leaving out: his country of Colombia. I am talking of Jim Emery, the son of Presbyterian Missionaries to Colombia where he grew up. He convinced me of the astounding beauty of the country and its importance for the Spanish Heritage in Latin America – religious, architectural, and military. It turned out he was not exaggerating; it was indeed significant. So, in the Spring months of 1975 my wife Keah and I traveled to and really got an impressive introduction to that country. I think the cartel and drug trade dangers had not started yet in any big way, but the country was living a hiatus between the "violencia" of the Liberal-Conservative war of the 1940s and 1950s and what was to come. We were, pardon the cliché, in the right place at the right time. Not to say it was not dangerous; it was, but for other reasons.

I would document the entire trip with hundreds of slides, many which would appear in the book. The story was told chronologically with these rubrics:

1. Medellín, Santa Fé de Antioquia and Bogotá
2. Crossing the Andes, Girardot, The Cauca Valley and Cali, Silvia and the Guambiano Indians, Popayán, and the San Agustín Civilization – Culture Archeological Site.
3. Beyond Bogotá: Tunja and Boyacá State, the Pantano de Vargas, the towns of Duitama, Sogamoso, Villa de Leiva, the "Ecce Homo" Monastery, Ráquira and Its Ceramics, and Zipaquirá and the Salt Cathedral.
4. Cartagena de Indias and the Fortifications and Churches, and lastly the Island of San Andrés, "Microcosm of the Caribbean."

One needs to see the book. I wish I could include the Table of Contents here; it explains it all. It tells not just the searching for the heritage but is loaded with anecdotes of travel by bus through the Andes at harrowing heights and next to deep ravines, and many humorous anecdotes of things and moments that simply happened. So, the narrative is very conversational and sprinkled with observations both serious and humorous of that country. Suffice to say, Keah and I were fortunate there were no mishaps; it could easily have been otherwise.

The book is indeed a wealth of information, a photographic record of the highlights of the Spanish Heritage and an important moment in our lives. Ironically in subsequent lectures in the SPA 472 course Colombia never did get the credit it deserves for one reason: the troubles had started, the battle between government and cartel with guerrillero warfare thrown in. Those years did not invite travel to Colombia by the inexperienced. A pity. And huge earthquakes damaged much of its grandeur in ensuing years. We never went back; Mexico, Guatemala, Honduras and the Mayas, and Brazil were the priorities. But I want to emphasize what a wonderful place Colombia was and potentially could be. At this writing I am "out of the loop" for current affairs, but from the Internet and Wikipedia I do not know if I would recognize much of what we saw and where we traveled.

I am going out on a bit of a limb: this book is fun and informative, and Colombia deserves it. An anecdote: years later, in 2014 when I was working as lecturer of things Brazilian on the National Geographic Explorer Ship after retirement from ASU, the former President of Colombia during the drug year troubles was aboard as a major guest lecturer. I dared strike up a conversation, gave him a copy of the book, a quick "gracias" and that was that. I did not expect him to read it but merely wanted to express my pleasure of his country and the book as a small thank you.

7

Travel, Research and Teaching in Guatemala and Mexico. In Quest of the Pre – Columbian Heritage. Volume 1. Guatemala. Trafford. Bloomington. 2013. 162 pp.

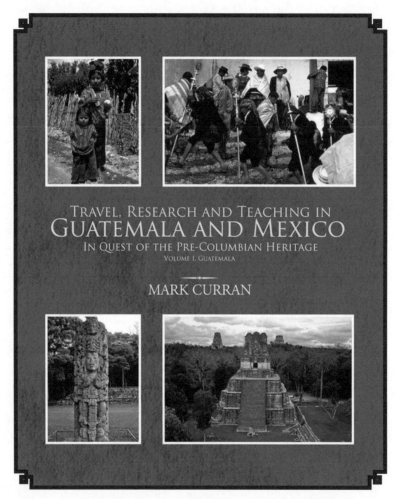

Travel, Teaching, Research in Guatemala

This book would now continue with much of the narrative style already introduced in "Adventures of a 'Gringo' Researcher in Brazil in the 1960s" and the Colombia book. I was beginning to get into the writing groove and model to be used in many subsequent books: the combination of travel diary notes, slides taken during the travels, and much preparation and research leading to description of the country, its cultural highlights and some at times naïve insights by the ole' professor. In three of these books to come, there is an additional component: writing of teaching in these countries, first as Director of the ASU Summer School in Guatemala in 1976 and 1977 and later in 1989 as Assistant Director of Professor Michael Flys' ASU Summer Program in Spain. In these cases, such notes and slides were used extensively in teaching SPA 472 Spanish American Civilization and to a much lesser extent, SPA 473 Civilization of Spain.

I can repeat what was said of the Colombia book. The narrative is not just research and study and travel notes but often as well memories, serious and humorous, of what happened, what we saw and experienced. I will say the situation in Guatemala was at times more somber, this due to the poverty of the Maya people and the devastating earthquake of 1976 and its aftermath. However, the wonderful Maya Heritage and Spanish Colonial Heritage survived and still reigned supreme.

The book tells the day-to-day travails of getting on a rickety city bus to teach at the Universidad Francisco Marroquín in Guatemala City, the nitty-gritty of late arriving books, rain dripping in the classrooms and some students giving their Guatemalan hosts big headaches. It was the outings outside the city which saved the day, i.e., Antigua, Puerto San José, El Lago de Atitlán, Tikal, and Copán in Honduras. The stars of the narrative are the Mayas themselves and their historic pre-Columbian sites of Tikal and Copán. There was a lot of tension in handling the summer school and young, impetuous students, but a lot of fun too at other moments. And a reunion with college best friend Eduardo Mathéu and his family at the family farm near Tecpán was an extra. He had a graduate degree from the University of Calfornia at Davis, learned all about apples, planted them successfully on the "finca" and had one named after him! Anecdotes of all appear as well as many photos documenting the country. Curran and wife enjoyed badly needed R and R later in the Yucatán with visits to the famous Maya-Toltec sites and some beach time at Isla

Mujeres. Once again, the style is conversational based on diaries. Also, the narrative covers both summers in Guatemala, 1976 and 1977.

A lengthy addendum to the book is the addition of Curran's research and classroom materials used to teach the matter in SPA Spanish American Civilization at Arizona State University

8

Travel, Research and Teaching in Guatemala and Mexico in Quest of the Pre – Columbian Heritage. Volume II. México. Trafford Publishing, Bloomington, 2013, 172 pp.

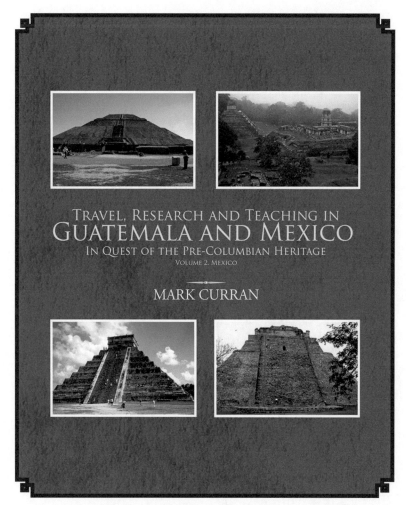

Travel, Teaching, Research. Vol. II. Mexico

Volume II's title is a bit of a misnomer because I did not teach in Mexico, but indeed the travel and research would lead to extensive use of the experience once again in the SPA 472 course at Arizona State University. After studying and teaching the topic for so many years, in 1998 an opportunity came to live and relive it all in a tour of Mexico with Grand Circle Tour company that filled in all the gaps! Although emphasis was on the most famous of archaeological sites in Mexico, as in Colombia, Guatemala and Honduras, the Spanish Heritage was experienced as well. One difference, there were no hassles or joys of herding students. It was just wife Keah and I that did the traveling. A short review of what we saw:

1. A wonderful introduction to the Pre – Columbian world of all Mexico at the Museo Nacional de Antropología e Historia in México, D.F. There is none better on the planet for this topic.
2. Teotihuacán – one of two "Proto-Cultura" sites in Mexico. The Teotihacanos
3. México D.F.: The Plaza Mayor and environs: the Toltec and later Aztec cultures
4. Monte Albán outside of Oaxaca and its neighbor Mitla
5. Palenque – the jewel of them all
6. Villa Hermosa, Parque – Museo de la Venta. "Proto – Cultura" for the Mayas to come
7. The Yucatán and the Classic and Post – Classic Sites of the Maya – Toltec Civilizations Chichén Itzá

Uxmal

Interspersed with it all were the modern, contemporary places where both Spanish (Mexican) and Indigenous cultures were so evident:

1. La Villa de Guadalupe and its importance to all Mexicans
2. The "frescos" of Diego Rivera and the 20th century role of José Guadalupe Posada, his woodcuts, the ballads of the "corridos," and the role of Frida Kahlo
3. Colonial Oaxaca: the churches, the plazas, the markets
4. San Cristóbal de las Casas and the Maya Heritage and modern battles to save the Indians and their property and culture. A scare at San Juan Chamula

5. Mérida the capital of colonial and modern Yucatán
6. Like Guatemala, a post trip R and R to famous new places: Cancún, Tulúm and Cozumel

It is quite a list and more than a mouthful. The narrative is once again based on research before, during and after the trip, but mainly on travel diaries as wife Keah and I obeyed the itinerary. The results once again were taught in that SPA Course until retirement in 2002 and at times beyond, part – time in the Spring until 2011. A few funny moments took place, but maybe not quite like previous books.

One frightening moment was when a San Juan Chamula Maya church guard, into his cups of "huaro" threatened us all with his nightstick inside the beautiful church. Unbeknownst to me cameras were not allowed and I along with other tourists snapped a few pictures, in my case without flash. The guard wanted the film from the camera, but I managed to escape the moment and we hurriedly climbed into the departure van. Just another day later there was another scary moment outside San Cristóbal de las Casas during the time of the Zapatista troubles and roadblocks on the highway by the Indians. Our guide Memo did a very un-Mexican thing – got us all up at the crack of dawn to travel the road before the Indians got the roadblock in place. It could have been interesting otherwise.

9

Portrait of Brazil in the Twentieth Century – The Universe of the "Literatura de Cordel." Trafford Publishing, Bloomington, 2013, 280 pp.

Portrait of Brazil in the 20th Century

I recall this book "went live" when I was aboard the National Geographic Explorer ship in 2013. It indeed did deserve better marketing and sales. I'm not sure in fact if anyone read it. In sum, it is the English version of the beautiful volume "Retrato do Brasil em Cordel" from São Paulo in 2011, already seen. Please see the entry of that volume for more details. Suffice to say, the text was reduced greatly although it is still a large book, the perhaps one hundred and fifty interior illustrations of photo-clichés and woodcuts from "Retrato" are missing (it would cost a fortune with Trafford to do them and the quality would not be up to snuff), but there is a photo gallery of the poets at the end. The photos are black and white, a bit fuzzy and again fewer than in "História do Brasil em Cordel" from USP. But, dear reader, it does TELL THE SAME STORY as "Retrato" but in English and less impressive surroundings.

So, why did I do it and what is its value? The answer is simple: it tells "cordel's" story in ENGLISH for ENGLISH LANGUAGE users. The cover photo is one of my favorites, taken by yours truly in the "Feira de São Cristóvão" in Rio's north zone perhaps in the 1980s. The poet is Apolônio Alves dos Santos, an excellent poet who was a highlight in "cordel" for perhaps 25 years, first in Brasília and then Rio. I write about him in various texts and used his story-poems in several of my books. Finally, I gave permission for the Library of Congress to use the photo (along with one of Azulão) for the Seminar on "Cordel" in the capital perhaps in 2011. So Apolônio and Azulão can be seen even if my book cannot!

The photo jogs my memory now and deserves more commentary: Apolônio is in his market stall at the fair, all his story-poems neatly arranged and ready for sale, and he looks neat as well. Aha! A fellow neatnik! To the rear one sees all the paraphernalia of a record-tape shop which was blaring music behind him, a curse and nemesis the poets battled for decades. Best is he displayed the story-poems as per the name of the genre "literatura de cordel" ["string literature"] as described from its beginnings in Portugal and many places of Brazil. "História do Brasil em Cordel" does as well. Once again, see the vignette of "Retrato do Brasil em Cordel" for the details.

Fifty Years of Research in Brazil – A Photographic Journey.
Trafford, Bloomington, 2014, 236 pp.

Fifty Years of Research on Brazil. A Photographic Journey

Ever busy, I decided to do yet another book on time spent in Brazil, but its essence being photographs (all taken by me from 1966 to 2013) recalling moments and people. I added prose vignettes describing people, places, and the times. Some were as short as a line or two, others up to a page or two. Trafford does a terrific job with cover and back cover images. Interior images may suffer from a less than desirable printing job, some better than others, some I wish I had back. All I know is my color slides looked like the cover images and were of the same quality. However, as I peruse the book to do this short description, I may protest too much. The interior photos accomplish their objective.

The book is divided into three parts: first, the poets, the publishers, market scenes over all the years; second, the intellectuals, informants, scholars, writers, friends and supporters of my efforts in Brazil; thirdly, photos of scenes of the folklore of the places visited over all those years. I daresay, many now are invaluable due to the fact the scene may have vanished from today's Brazil, a case in point the woodburning sternwheelers of the São Francisco Navigation Company on the same river up to the end of the 1960s.

Returning to the book after eight years, I am proud of it, my efforts, but mainly the historic value of what is documented. Photos and slides are different from photo-clichés and woodcuts, however, the former really tell the story well.

Suffice to see my cover choice:

The poets in the left-hand column: Manoel Camilo dos Santos, Rodolfo Coelho Cavalcante, Abraão Batista and Marcelo Soares.

In the center: scenes of the "bonecos de barro" [clay dolls of Caruarú], the "saveiro" or small craft sail boats of Salvador, Bahia and the "recôncavo," unloading cotton or jute bales at the old, now gone docks of the Mercado Modelo in Salvador, and a picture of the "gaiolas" or sternwheelers on the São Francisco River.

The column to the right: Curran with Ariano Suassuna, Jorge Amado, Raquel de Queirós and Plínio Martins.

Dear reader, I can't begin to mention all that is of value in these photos. If you are so moved, the book is on Amazon.com and of course on the Trafford web page at Trafford.com. I'm not angling for sales; I'm providing you with an opportunity to see memorable moments of Brazil.

The author rests his case.

11

Travel and Teaching in Portugal and Spain – a Photographic Journey. Trafford, Bloomington, 2014, 297 pp.

Travel and Teaching in Portugal and Spain - A Photographic Journey

Following the model now of books on Colombia, Guatemala, and Mexico, this book combines the detailed diary of our summer in Portugal and Spain with the concept of using my slides to the utmost to show what we experienced and saw. The trip was my first to the "metropoli" of both Portugal and Spain, long overdue one may say. The occasion was in 1987 as an "assistant" professor to Dr, Michael Flys, Director for years of the ASU Summer School in Spain.

Although now with three decades of teaching of Brazil and diverse countries and cultures of Spanish America in literature and civilization courses (and language courses in the early years), and although I had specialized in Golden Age Spanish Literature in graduate school, this was the first opportunity to get to "my roots." A bit different, both daughter Katie and wife Keah were along on the trip and probably saved the day. We socialized in those days with the Flys, Michael, Felisa (from Cuenca), and daughters Katie and Tamara played together at diverse times.

We the Currans went to the Peninsula early with the motive of spending about three weeks in Portugal to see tourist highlights, experience Portuguese culture and whenever possible report on the famous history, literature, and religious foundation for what the Portuguese discovers and colonizers brought to Brazil. We were on a limited budget, thus did not stay at the famous "pousadas," but rather in perhaps 3-star hotels. Sometimes there was icy water in the showers, sometimes breakfast was a joke, the beds squeaked, but we learned some basic travel "ropes" and gradually had tasty dining, were introduced to the light, fizzy "vinho verde" and many ice creams for Katie. And I forgot, enjoyed the Portuguese version of Brazil's "cafezinho," the "bica."

There were many highlights; I can't retell the large book but the cliché of "Castles in Spain" was just as true in Portugal. The "Mosteiro" in Belém with the tombs of Vasco da Gama, Camões, and perhaps King Sebastião was a first highlight; others to follow were the "azulejo" museum and "fado" in Lisboa, all three castles of Sintra, the walled city of Óbidos, the gigantic medieval Cistercian monastery in Alcobaça, windmills which must have been the same in Don Quixote's day, the beautiful ocean experience at Nazaré, the shrine at Fátima, the famous church of Batalha, the famous northern cities but especially Coimbra and its Medieval University. I absorbed and photographed anything to do with Portugal's history and its famous poet Luís de Camões and all those churches. Mission accomplished.

We did not go to southern Portugal to the Algarve mainly since beaches were not the main goal and there was a time constraint. I constantly was mentally making notes of comparison to the Brazil I knew so well and can say Portugal was as it should have been. Oh, the spoken Portuguese was a challenge, so different from that of Brazil, but if I said, "Fale devagar por favor," [speak slowly please], that generally did the trick. They sometimes thought I was from southern Brazil. What can I say? Katie and Keah were good troopers.

We traveled then by bus across the eastern-southern part of Portugal into southern Spain, Andalucía and our base city Málaga where we would meet the Flys' and the students. Now Professor Flys was in charge for sure, but also had the "headaches" of herding young college students with high hormones and a penchant to drink and party into all hours of the night, many nights.

Churches, more churches, castles, and History! I was well prepared in general details of Spanish history, culture, art and especially literature. Once again here are the highlights in Málaga the first part of the Summer School: the Cathedral of Málaga for openers with its black Christ, Corpus Christi celebration, the huge silver "Custodia" or Monstrance for the Corpus Christi procession (just a bit like Holy Week in Sevilla), the pebble covered, icy water beach of Torremolinos, but then the terrific "feria" of Málaga with the ladies dancing "sevillanas" in their flamenco dresses and the Arabian Horses in the street parades. And our first bullfight, a disappointing affair because it was the students and "student" bulls as well.

Then things really got exciting: the "gira" of Andalucía (Professor Flys did not miss a trick): Córdoba and the "Mesquita," Granada and the Alhambra, Sevilla and its Cathedral and the "Giralda" and "Alcázar" and a first-rate flamenco show. I add that here and all over Spain I was clued into the major figures of Spanish Literature and Painting as they and they cities would come up, suffice to mention Luis de Góngora of Córdoba, Federico García Lorca of Granada, and one of the great romantic poets as well.

71

As I try to summarize it all, I can't. See the book which is very large out of necessity and all the great stuff I can't get to here. Names, places, events, ups and downs, all important.

Then we began the long "gira" to central and northwest Spain and more unforgettable highlights, among them: the Roman Ruins of Mérida, the medieval university city of Salamanca and all its churches. Now we were getting into the territory of many of the classics of Spanish Literature I had studied: the "Lazarillo de Tormes" novel of Salamanca, the poet Garcilaso de la Vega of "Eclogue" fame, the hugely important Fray Luis de León was Garcilaso's teacher at the University of Salamanca ("Vida Retirada,)" one of the most famous poems of the Golden Age. Later we would see the vestiges of the Spanish "mystics," Santa Teresa de Jesús and San Juan de la Cruz in Ávila and Segovia. And of modern fame the irascible and powerful 20th century Rector of the University, iconoclast Miguel de Unamuno. I was in literary heaven. And the students were in party heaven night after night. So much I'm leaving out! Ay!

Things farther north were just as great, first the medieval city of Santiago de Compostela, the pilgrimage route from France, the much-remodeled centuries old Cathedral with all the architectural changes, the "Botafumeiro" [the "mother" of all Incense Boats] that puts all others to shame (to hide the stench of the pilgrims they said) and a refreshing light treat, Spain's version of "vinho verde." "Ribeiro Claro" wine and "Caldo Gallego" sustained us, or least some of us. The singing university students, the famous Tunas entertained us and joined the party.

Professor Flys hauled us on a one - day bus trip to the Rías or Fjords of Spain south of Santiago de Compostela. It was gorgeous and we were sorry to leave. Better things ahead: the city of León one of the main cities on the Camino de Santiago and half a dozen historic churches from the Romanesque, Gothic, you name it. The Cathedral was best: the most stained glass of any church in Spain (and that is an understatement), comparable they said to Chartres. One small note: one of my teaching colleagues on the trip from another school in Phoenix and I returned to the Cathedral, this after imbibing way too much of the local tasty "clarete." These churches have a nice echo; I was inspired to chant a few bars of Gregorian Chant (I don't know Gregorian

Chant), then whistle the same before the sacristan arrived and kicked us out. Query? Were we the first and last? Just maybe.

Now we were headed back down to Madrid via Valladolid, Simancos Castle, Ávila. In the latter we saw the old medieval stone walls and then Santa Teresa de Jesus's Church with the museum alongside and one of her fingers with an emerald ring in a jar of formaldehyde. Hmm. I forgot to mention the Paradores and such we saw along the way.

Now to the location of Part II of the Summer School – Madrid. A huge and amazing place. I can just make a list; there is so much. Literature: Cervantes, Lope de Vega and Calderón de la Barca for openers! Each item is a story told in the book and doing this now takes me back. A long time ago in España! I'll add "verbetes" as necessary when they come to mind!

The statues of Don Quixote, Sancho, and Rocinante in the Plaza de España,

just statues but a huge slice of Mark's studies and teaching at ASU.

La Gran Vía – the main avenue downtown, one side street leading to the Plaza Mayor. We remember the McDonald's close by where we got ice cream.

Oh, our favorite eating spot in Madrid was a tip from my Mormon student Joe – a Chinese restaurant with aquariums with tropical fish, but a chicken dinner with rice and veggies that was reminiscent of our fried chicken. And you got a bottle of wine with the meal. And I remember it was QUIET! Not an easy thing in Madrid, probably our favorite food there.

La Plaza Mayor y las Cuevas. Las Cuevas is famous for all the Spanish "Tapas," most of which did not agree with me. Pimientos, fishy stuff, but always a glass of wine.

Cerámica de Lladró. Because we did not agree to buy nine year old Katie a real flamenco dress (maybe $200), the Lladró of El Greco and a small girl dancing flamenco were the main souvenirs of the trip. Katie will inherit the dancing girl someday (she does not want it now).

"Guitarras de concierto." I wish I knew the name of the shop, but I played a wonderful full-toned Spanish Classic guitar. In heaven. I remember a very artistic looking Spaniard, coifed long hair, upper-class clothing, picking up a guitar and playing it. He I think played in a flamenco hall. The gorgeous classic guitar Mark was allowed to play would have been $5000 at the time.

Avenida Castellanos – how many lanes? A dozen. The main way into and out of Madrid.

El Parque del Buen Retiro – somewhere I have a copy of the painting of the noble who owned it and later donated it to the city of Madrid. There were Zarzuela performances which I did not understand. Rowboats on the lake. This is a scene from the past of performances of plays by Lope and Calderón de la Barca.

El Prado and the huge "salones" – El Greco, Velázquez, and Goya. See the book for some examples, but the Prado had all copyrights, and you could take no pictures. I bought commercial slides for use back home but in this book once again those present copyright problems. The ones included are those I took later with a digital camera in the NYC Museum of Art. Permissions granted.

The Palacio Real in Madrid. Spain's "Versailles," gloriously decadent. Los Borbones. (The Hapsburgs would be in Felipe II's huge El Escorial.) El Museo de Armas.

Then came the one-day trip to famous Toledo.

View of Toledo. The bus stopped, we got out and marveled at this famous scene where El Greco did one of his most famous paintings.

"La Catedral inmensa." It was here we saw the "Custodia de Oro" of outlandish size, gold, and silver, for the Benediction of the Holy Sacrament at Mass and the religious processions throughout the year. I have slides. It is made of many, many kilos of gold and more of silver. A smaller version, but no less beautiful we saw in Popayán, Colombia, made of jewels and gold and stored in a Bank Vault except for the occasional procession. It had the two Hapsburg Eagles with the sacred host in the middle and all surrounded with emeralds, and of course gold.

La Casa del Greco. Fine, but we saw more of his paintings in the Prado.

The famous Synagogues. Wonderful. Sinagoga del Tránsito. The Jews in Toledo had a period of peace with old Spain and the Catholics, a bit like Granada with the Moslems and the Christians and the Jews, ie. Maimónides, Averrroes. It all had to do with Jewish banking and handling the finances of the Crown. Alas, it did not last – 1492!

San Juan de los Reyes

Damasceno goldwork and Toledo swords

The Trip to Segovia

The famous "Alcázar" Castle-Palace. One of the most famous and best of all Spain, "kitsch" – they say the Disneyland Castle is modeled on it. Huge, scary tall, and wonderful gallery up on top of Spanish weapons.

The Roman Aqueduct – beautifully preserved and used until recent times. The Roman presence is all over Spain and was essential in its history.

The church and tomb of San Juan de la Cruz. We ran into this church by accident, off on our own after the group did the usual stuff. San Juan along with Santa Teresa the "mystics of Spain." "The Dark Night of the Soul" in Literature.

The Día de Campo and Huge Jug of Wine. A wonderful mountain stream, a picnic with all kinds of food Michael acquired, and perhaps a five-gallon jug of the local wine to wash it down. A good time was had by all.

The Curran's Private Visit to the Religious Sites – the "Santuarios" [Sanctuaries]

Passing by Cervantes' birthplace

Zaragoza and the Basílica de la Virgen del Pilar. Connection to St. James, "Santiago Matamoros"

Barbastro and Opus Dei

France and Lourdes

San Sebastián and Basque Country

The surprise of Aspeitia-Loyola and St. Ignacio Loyola's castle and Basílica and Mark's Jesuit Education Roots

Burgos, the City Gate, and the Cathedral, the Tombs of El Cid y Doña Ximena. Locked in, the bus horn honks, keys from the sacristan. Close call.

Last but not least

El Escorial. The huge, foreboding edifice of Felipe II

Valle de los Caídos [Valley of the Fallen] and Franco's Mausoleum

Party days at the café in the Colegio Mayor

    Kt and Tamara dancing Sevillanas

    Jacinto who kept us fed and watered for that time.

.

TWA home. There were a whopping 297 pages and none worthy of leaving out. Ups and downs. Many joys and a few sorrows. Blank pages of Spanish history and literature were filled in. Now I can teach SPA 473 – "Civilización de España."

The cover images: on the left from top to bottom,

Portugal:

The Monument to the Discoverers – Belém

The Medieval Cistercian Monastery of Alcobaça

The Medieval Walled City of Óbidos

The Gothic Church of Batalha

The cover images on the right from top to bottom:

One of the main rooms of the Alhambra Palace

The Stained Glass Marvels of the Cathedral of León

The Castle of Segovia

The Stained-Glass Window of Castille-León

12

Relembrando – a Velha Literatura de Cordel e a Voz dos Poetas. Trafford, Bloomington, 2014, 296 pp.

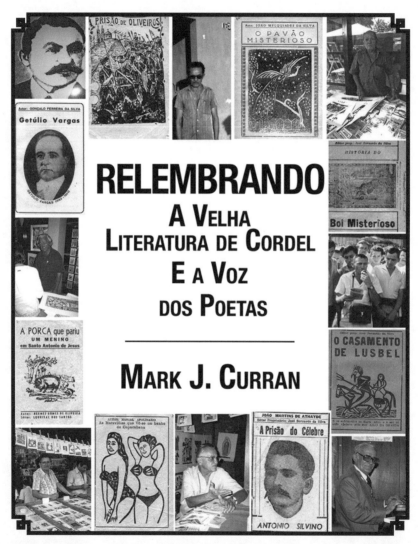

Relembrando – A Velha Literatura de Cordel e a Voz dos Poetas

This large tome is of course a return to research topics. I decided to include the original "Literatura de Cordel" book from Brazil since it was long ago out of print. Unbeknownst to me, someone copied it to the Internet. But the large portion of this new book was the series of written interviews with "cordel" poets done in the late 1970s and never published. Most of the important poets of "Cordel" participated, and the interviews are published only here. .

THE POETS AND PUBLISHERS THAT RESPONDED TO THE QUESTIONAIRE, IN ALPHABETICAL ORDER, NUMBERED 1 – 40.

1. Manuel D'Almeida Filho
2. José Marques de Andrade
3. Teófilo de Azevedo Filho
4. Abraão Bezerra Batista
5. Otacílio *Batista*
6. Paulo Nunes Batista
7. José Francisco Borges
8. João Bandeira de Caldas
9. Pedro Bandeira de Caldas
10. Elias Alves Carvalho
11. Rodolfo Coelho Cavalcante
12. Antônio Ribeiro Conceição
13. José Severino Cristóvão
14. José Cunha Neto
15. José Cavalcanti e Ferreira (Dila)
16. João Carneiro Fontenele Filho
17. José Costa Leite
18. Carolino Leobas
19. Augusto Souza de Lima
20. João de Lima
21. José Tomás de Lima
22. Franklin Cerqueira de Machado
23. José Vicente do Nascimento
24. João Crispim Ramos
25. Alípio Bispo dos Santos
26. Apolônio Alves dos Santos
27. Erotildes Miranda dos Santos
28. José João dos Santo (Azulão)
29. Manoel Camilo dos Santos
30. Valeriano Félix dos Santos
31. Alberto Porfírio da Silva
32. Benoni Conrado da Silva
33. Expedito F. da Silva
34. João Vicente da Silva
35. José Ferreira da Silva
36. José Francisco da Silva
37. Manoel Caboclo e Silva
38. Minelvino Francisco Silva
39. José Soares
40. Francisco Peres de Souza

Thus, the book is in Portuguese. I don't know if anyone ever read it. I love the image choices for the cover:

The poets (clockwise from upper left): Leandro Gomes de Barros, Manoel Camilo dos Santos, José Costa Leite, José João dos Santos (Azulão), Rodolfo Coelho Cavalcante, J. Borges, Apolônio Alves dos Santos, and Abraão Batista.

The "cordel" covers and titles, some of the most famous of the genre.

13

It Happened in Brazil – Chronicle of a North American Researcher
in Brazil II. Trafford. Bloomington, 2015, 302 pp.

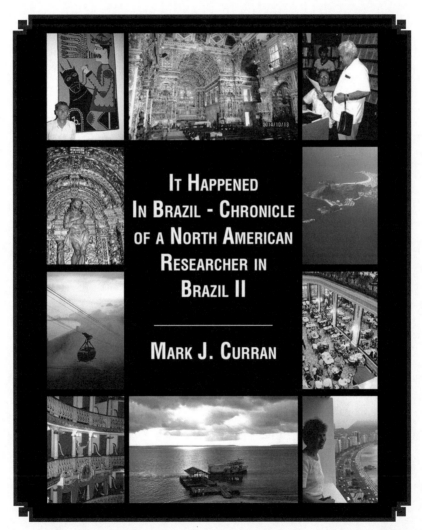

It Happened in Brazil – Chronicle of a North American Researcher in Brasil II

It is now back to the memory books, some both in Portuguese and English, yours truly thinking it might be of interest to both Brazilians and to English speakers. Ha! I doubt anyone but me read it. This is one more in the series "Stories I Told My Students." The title is inspired by my favorite modern writer in Brazil, Luís Fernando Veríssimo known for his clever, sometimes hilarious short "crônicas" or vignettes of everyday life in Brazil. I must have a dozen of his books and used them extensively in the final years of teaching at ASU. I did my own "crônicas."

The book is liberally sprinkled with all the photographs of those many research trips to Brazil from 1969 to 1985. There are many good moments, some not so good. It is worthwhile just to mention here each trip, its purpose, and a highlight or two.

> 1969. Recife. M's book "A Literatura de Cordel" accepted and ramrodded by no less than Ariano Suassuna. "Kardecismo" in Campina Grande. Mark in Rio
>
> 1970. Mark and Keah in Brazil, second honeymoon**
>
> 1973. Mark and the first big Congress on "Camões," hilarious tales of the Portuguese and others at this first Congress. FCRB "Estudos" book out; big break for Mark
>
> 1978. Mark in Rio. Many moments, anecdotes and "crônicas." Eventful.
>
> 1981. Mark in Bahia, research moments on Cuíca and Rodolfo. Mark to Recife, depressing, peddling studies.
>
> 1981. November. Mark to Bahia. 50 Years of Literature of Jorge Amado, Mark's small book. Another highlight of all the times in Brazil.
>
> 1985. Mark in Brazil. Summer. A low time, no publications, battle to get Cuíca and Rodolfo books out. Some relief: Air Pass for the first time to São Paulo and Rio Grande do Sul in the south. All new for Mark

1985. November. A great trip. Mark and Keah back in Brazil, the Sebastião Nunes Batista Prize and travel to the interior of São Paulo. Mark and Keah then enjoy the great Air Pass to Bahia (see old friends Mário and Laís) and incredible time in Manaus and the Hotel Rio Negro and the Amazon.

14

Aconteceu no Brasil – Crônicas de um Pesquisador Norte-Americano no Brasil II. Trafford. Bloomington, 2015, 276 pps.

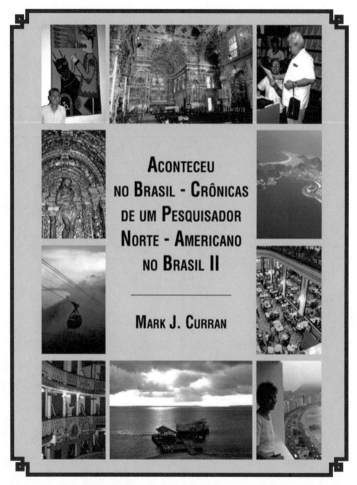

Aconteceu no Brasil – Crônicas de um Pesquisador Norte-Americano no Brasil II

This is the Portuguese version of n. 13.

15

Diary of a North American Researcher in Brazil III. Trafford. Bloomington, 2016, 230 pp.

Diary of a North American Researcher in Brazil III

This book continues in the fashion of "It Happened in Brazil II," already seen. Basically, it is bringing up to date research and travel in Brazil to the end in 2005 and is the last book in the series "Stories I Told My Students." In addition, it is a "thank you" to the poets, the intellectuals, informants, and to the friends who supported me in good times and bad, happy and some sad, until the end of active research in that country. The future will hold other trips to Brazil, but unrelated to research and later to the present, the new "odyssey" of creating cultural, historical fiction from it all. Let's list the years and the events.

1988.

Invitation to the "Conference on Northeastern Literature" in Recife. The moment was a modern tribute to Gilberto Freyre's famous 1926 Conference on Northeastern Regionalism and Literature. And it was an effort to meet old friends and make some new ones. It started with an encounter with Henrique and Cristina Kerti who hosted me throughout the years. The same was true with now married Flávio Veloso, his wife and child Mirtes. Flávio was a great friend in 1966 and his father Admiral Veloso helped me exit Brazil's bureaucracy in 1967. Another encounter was with Hélio Coelho a friend and "cicerone" of those days.

The conference itself was wonderful with outstanding moments of Ariano Suassuna, now an icon of northeastern culture, meeting and conversing with Raquel de Queiróz, an icon from the Novel of the Northeast in the 1920s to the present, a very humbling moment when my formal talk was scheduled and followed one of Ariano's heralded "espetáculo" presentations. Another "notch in the research revolver" was finally meeting Liedo Maranhão, a huge voice in recording and chronicling the old São José Market and its denizens in the mid-20th century.

Moving on to a short visit in Bahia there was an encounter with friends, "cicerones" Edilene Matos and Carlos Cunha of the whole Bahia odyssey and books already seen. Equally important was the reunion with Mário and Laís Barros (we met at ASU in the early 1970s when Mário studied electrical engineering); they saved my "social" life in Brazil for perhaps three decades.

1989. Travel to Brazil for an Invited Talk at the University of Paraíba in João Pessoa and a reunion with colleague Neuma Fechine Borges. She and her husband hosted me, socialized with me, took me to the local sites, and eventually arranged a meeting with Átila de Almeida in Campina Grande, owner of the largest and best private "cordel" connection in Brazil.

On this trip it is the people encountered that matter. After João Pessoa there were important moments in Rio. I met with the Kertis at the great salon in the old Hotel Glória with the Pedro II empire furniture. Then with Maria Eduarda Lessa, wife of deceased Orígenes who allowed me to do copious reading and then xeroxing of his collection which would be instrumental in being able to write "História do Brasil em Cordel." In Rio I took the "bonde" [electric cable car] of "Black Orpheus" fame to Santa Teresa and met General Umberto Peregrino the principal patron of "cordel" then in Rio de Janeiro. And there was a brief meeting and perusal of the "cordel" collection of Ivan Cavalcanti Proença with a sentimental, seminal link to all the work in Brazil. His father was reformed army Colonel Manuel Cavalcanti Proença who first mentored me on "cordel" in Brazil, the moment ending with his heart attack and sudden death in December 1966. I forgot, there was a stop in Bahia before the Conference and a wonderful reunion with Edilene and Carlos.

1990 Brazil. Research and Tourism

I was again with Edilene and Carlos in Bahia and dealing with the preparation of the book on Cuíca de Santo Amaro at the Jorge Amado Foundation. And there much nostalgic tourism in Salvador, all the famous old city sites already mentioned.

In João Pessoa I hopped a bus to the interior, remembering 1966, to Campina Grande where I finally met Átila Almeida, perused his famous, huge collection and stayed up until 2:00 a.m. feverously reading and taking notes on perhaps two dozen important story-poems that would be instrumental in "História do Brasil em Cordel." Átila was what the Brazilians call "boa prosa," a great conversationalist and raconteur. He was quite ill but still enjoyed his "doses" [snorts] of cachaça from a huge jug he bought in the market and lugged up the hill to his home. Great hospitality by him and his wife. This meeting was our only one.

Again with that great Varig "Air Pass," this time on a whim from João Pessoa to Rio and a transfer to a plane to Paraná State and finally to the "Cataratas de Iguaçu." Unforgettable. I have not been to Niagara Falls, but the Cataracts would win hands down.

1990. Brazil again. November. Bahia

The falderal and book party for the publication, finally, of "Cuíca de Santo Amaro Poeta-Repórter da Bahia." The story is already told earlier in this narrative.

1996. Brazil

A highlight was the encounter with former ASU student Roberto Froelich in Rio de Janeiro. We had some beery times recalling the good old days, got caught up, and Roberto took me to new tourist sites in Rio and Niterói. And another unforgettable moment: the two of us playing classic guitar in a shop in downtown Rio. Once again, Roberto not only hosted me in his modest apartment, but saved my life socially. And there were wonderful moments when we just talked of language, literature and the great works of Spain, Spanish America, and Brazil. Thank you, Roberto.

Then I moved on to São Paulo to give a talk at a meeting at USP (a minor event but it paid for the trip). A far more important moment was with Sérgio Miceli and signing the contract for "História do Brasil em Cordel." There was a new and brief friendship with Abigail and Zé Rubens who hosted me for a few days, vis a vis their contact with Clarice Deal the Portuguese teacher at ASU. Then a new and memorable "cordel" moment in São Paulo – being with and witnessing poet Téo Azevedo and his great radio show on Rádio Atual in the far suburbs, but meeting not only more "cordel" poets and "cantadores" but being introduced to the singing phenomenon of the northeast – the "boiadas" akin to cowboy yodeling in the U.S. And last, but not least, meeting Michael Grossman who introduced me to that milieu at the "Consulado Mineiro" a local bar. Michael was teaming up with Téo Azevedo to do a mixture of "cantoria" and blues; one participant was the harmonica player of the "Blues Etílicos," then the most famous pop music group in São Paulo and maybe all Brazil. Uh oh. I forgot. Yet another memorable moment when I took subway after subway to meet Assis Angelo, the kingpin of Northeastern Culture in all São Paulo with a radio – TV show that reached a few million people! Gracious, we drank some beer at a "pé sujo" and shared our lives, he telling me the entire story of migrating from the Northeast and how it all turned out for the best in the metropolis.

Brazil 2000. The BRASA [Brazilian Studies Association] meeting in Recife and life-long memory

I landed in Rio, had another great encounter with Robero Froelich now enthused over Bloom's "The Western Canon" and we did that reminiscing again. This was the trip when I got on the wrong bus back to my hotel and ended up climbing up hill and through the famous and perhaps notorious "favela," Rocinha. Getting to know Rio! There was a sad but not sad reunion with Cristina Kerti, friend Henrique recently deceased with heart trouble. The good: we met at her restaurant and had a wonderful meeting with daughter and her husband. Cristina made sure I had the best of "aperitivos, churrasco e sobremesa." Thank you, Cristina.

On to Recife, but via Salvador. I basically did tourism once again to the old standbys – the Praça da Sé, Igreja de São Francisco, the Pelourinho, visiting Myriam Fraga. And there was time with Edilene and Carlos, but "cordel" in Bahia was not the same since Rodolfo died in 1986 and my Cuíca book came out in 1990.

Arrival in Recife. Mark, how things have changed. Lodging for the BRASA meeting was in a luxury high-rise 20 story hotel, and Boa Viagem looked more like a straight-lined Copacabana than those "good old days." Of note, the air conditioning in the hotel, a la "brasileiro," was cold enough to freeze water and my room until I finally figured out the new high-tech thermostat. Oh, I had developed the mother of all colds, the works. Throat lozenges and a mild antibiotic (you don't need a RX prescription in Brazil, and I knew what I needed.) helped but it took three or four days.

This was what, now, the fourth or fifth conference in Brazil, but the first for BRASA, so it was a big deal. The opening night was by bus to the Universidade Federal de Pernambuco and the freezing auditorium (I had my chamois shirt buttoned at the neck with the collar up and still had to go out to the lobby to warm up.) The northeastern cultural ICON Ariano Suassuna was there with his wife, but I noticed they left early. The air conditioning? I heard the original Quinteto Violado of national fame, heard them play "Disparada" another all-time favorite by Geraldo Vandré and recorded by Jair Rodrigues. But the performance was also very Brazilian, the sound was deafening. I think they could have turned it down by 2/3 and it might have been okay.

The highlight of the meeting for me, and perhaps for many of the trips to Brazil was when I read my paper to a smiling, laughing and applauding Ariano Suassuna. There's a story: I had ripped up my formal talk (unhappy memories of 1990 at UFEPE) and decided to just tell anecdotes of that first research experience in Recife and the Northeast in 1966. And stories of the disingenuous "gringo" trying to figure out Brazil. It WAS funny. Idelette Mozart, chair of the session and Ph.D. from the Sorbonne said, "Mark, write that up and send it to me. We will publish it right away." (I forgot where.). Hmm. I seem to be familiar with this drill. I did not do that but want to say the talk became the "genesis" of a similar wonderfully received talk in São Paulo (to come) and the future book "Adventures of a 'Gringo' Researcher in Brazil in the 1960s – In search of 'Cordel.'"

There's more: at lunch that day Ariano Suassuna came up to me and gave a heartening "thank you" for the opportunity to use the interviews from "A Literatura de Cordel" in his novel "A Pedra do Reino." He basically said, "I never got a chance to thank you." Well, curious reader, that was more icing on the cake of all the work, tribulations, and good times in Brazil up to that moment, that along with the moments with Jorge Amado.

After that, the meeting was a slow fade. Two moments: I heard some of the best music (for my taste) in Brazil since 1966 – the Northeastern orchestra of Sá Grama, in one of the old baroque churches of Olinda, and met a person who indeed became more important later, young Chris Dunn a graduate of Brown in 1994. Another moment, exciting for most was visiting the vast art works of Francisco Brennand, a colleague of Ariano's back in those 1950 and 1960 days. I was told one of his paintings could bring one MILLION dollars in 2000. I enjoyed the music far more.

2001. São Paulo. "Cem Anos de Cordel"

The good moments now keep coming. Josph Luyten had a long-time correspondence with me and knowing and liking my writing, invited me to be one of the principal speakers at a huge event in São Paulo – "Cem Anos de Cordel" [One Hundred Years of 'Cordel'"]. Folks, I am now on a "roll" after those difficult years in the mid-1980s.

It was this trip when I finally met Joseph Luyten (we had corresponded for years), the renowned Audálio Dantas (and we became good friends), and reencountered or met anew the "greats" of "cordel" of the era. Read my account, there are many wonderful moments, Azulão, Marcelo Soares and especially J. Borges. The background was the "Pavão Misterioso," Padre Cicero, Lampião, Carlos Magno all portrayed in art. The highlight was the exhibition of the best from Joseph Luyten's collection, story- poems dating from Leandro Gomes de Barros and the teens of the 20th century, João Martins de Atayde, and dozens of others. My talk, an improved version of that of 2000 in Recife, drew a packed room and was full of jokes and laughter. At the end of 45 minutes Curator Audálio said, "Go on, go on." So, I did very successfully for about another 15 minutes. (As mentioned, this talk was the genesis for the book "Adventures of a 'Gringo Researcher in Brazil in the 1960s - In Search of the 'Literatura de Cordel.'") Incidentally, many copies of "História do Brasil em Cordel" were on the table and a lot of autographs were signed.

On the way home from São Paulo I had fun again with Roberto Froelich in Rio and then took a deep breath and called Glória Pérez of "telenovela" fame on TV Globo, met her in the most beautiful apartment I have ever seen – all glass overlooking Copacabana AND Leblon. The subject was a story-poem telling of the death of her daughter by the TV and real-life villain of the soap opera, a tragedy for her and Brazil.

How could Brazil get better? It did not in terms of conferences and trips, but yes with publications. I had talked to Plínio Martins in São Paulo in 2001 and the wheels were turning for "Retrato do Brasil em Cordel." Only problem, it took ten years.

Brazil, 2002. Taking the Manuscript and "Cordel" Illustrations to Plínio Martins.

The mission was accomplished in São Paulo with the successful delivery of the materials. Then I "paid the rent" with a talk at a very unimpressive and disappointing conference at USP. Emotionally, I was tired and for the first time, left Brazil early to come home. This should tell the reader something. I was thinking of the retirement soon to come from ASU.

Brazil, 2005. Final Trip to Brazil before Retirement.

As usual there were many motives for the trip. The expenses would be covered because of an invited talk at a Conference in João Pessoa, to be seen.

But there were other motives: travel to São Paulo to Ateliê Editorial and trying to save the day for "Retrato." There was a very amicable talk with Plínio Martins who explained the slowness (200 books at Ateliê) and "editing" of the huge Mss. In addition, there was a reencounter with Audálio Dantas at the State of Folk Art Fair of São Paulo, a huge and beautiful affair.

There was a brief stop in Rio and once again a fun encounter with Roberto Froelich.

Then I headed north to Bahia, a nostalgic "goodbye" to the old city, and to old friends Mário and Laís Barros.

Finally, to the Conference in João Pessoa. It is worthwhile reading to see my report and photos. The paper was the least of it all. They like "100 Anos" had set up a "northeastern fair" and all the poets displayed their works. Of note, there was yet another meeting with Marcelo Soares, but most important, finally with José Costa Leite, one of the old "greats." And my hostess was old friend, Neuma Fechine Borges. She finally received the honor she always deserved in Paraíba at that meeting. On the return flight to São Paulo and then home to Phoenix, there was a lot of "nostalgia" thinking of all these years, but now official first retirement from ASU and plans for the future (strangely enough, they did not include all these books). I was thinking of doing music again in restaurants in Durango, Colorado, teaching in the summer at Fort Lewis College in Durango, and enjoying the family with hiking, fishing, and living with friends in Colorado and at church in Bayfield.

16

Diário de um Pesquisador Norte Americano no Brasil III

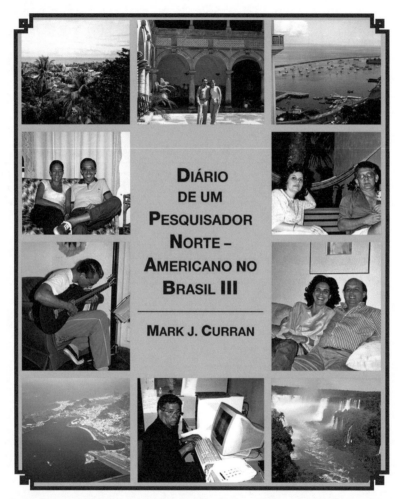

DIÁRIO DE UM PESQUISADOR NORTE – AMERICANO NO BRASIL III

MARK J. CURRAN

Diário de um Pesquisador Norte-Americano no Brasil III

This is the Portuguese language version of number 23.

17

Letters from Brazil a Cultural Historical Narrative Made Fiction. Trafford, Bloomington, 2017, 204 pp.

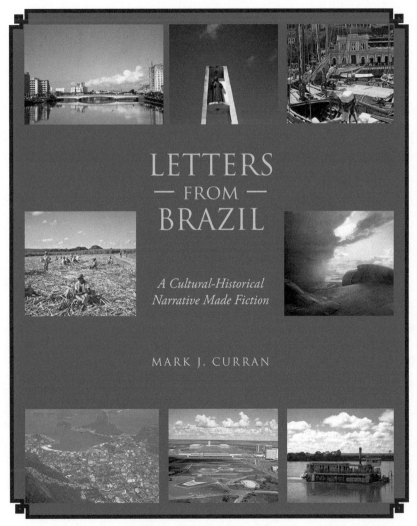

Letters from Brazil I

This book marks the first venture into fiction, albeit what I call "a cultural-historical narrative made fiction." Believe me, it was not easy, and I took baby steps in this first effort. The book is based upon the entire year of research and living in Brazil in 1966 – 1967 and the non-fiction account already seen: "Adventures of a 'Gringo' Researcher in Brazil in the 1960s – In Search of the 'Literatura de Cordel.'"

From the back cover,

"Letters from Brazil: A Cultural-Historical Narrative Made Fiction" recounts the adventures of young researcher Mike Gaherty in Brazil in the turbulent 1960s. It tells the story of his research on Brazilian folklore and folk – popular literature (with inevitable amorous moments along the way) while dodging encounters and threats from agents of the DOPS, Brazil's chief espionage, anti-communist, and anti-subversion agency. The nation's military revolution of 1964 and subsequent evolution to dictatorship are the background for Gaherty's ups and downs in Brazil's Northeast, the Northeast Interior, Salvador da Bahia, Rio de Janeiro, Brasília, the Amazon, and a final harrowing time in Recife.

"The thread of the narrative is the series of letters requested of Gaherty by James Hansen of the New York Times (International Section) and his later involvement with Stanley Iverson of the INR (Bureau of Intelligence and Research of the United States Department of State – WHA (Western Hemisphere Affairs) reporting on Gaherty's own research activities and his discoveries of political and social sentiment in northeastern Brazil. The young American researcher reports as well on meetings with major Brazilian cultural figures, encounters with Brazilian Afro-Brazilian phenomena like Xangô, Candomblé, and Capoeira, impressive times during New Year's Eve and the Carnival in Rio de Janeiro, and cultural-travel highlights throughout Brazil. The fly in the ointment was the DOPS.

A Professor Takes to the Sea I

Learning the Ropes on the National Geographic Explorer.

Volume I. "Epic South America" 2013.

Trafford Publishing, Bloomington, 2018, 193 pp.

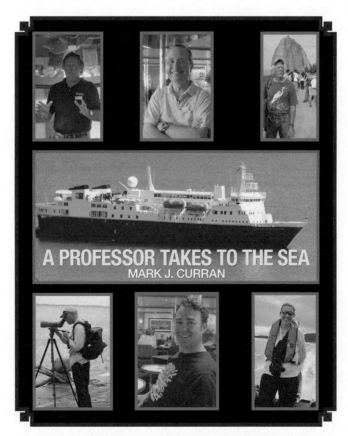

A Professor Takes to the Sea I

A return to non – fiction, this book tells the story of a wonderful retirement adventure in 2013 as a cultural lecturer on the National Geographic Explorer ship via Lindblad Expeditions. It was almost too good to be true. Jen Martin, the person in charge of recruiting staff and speakers for LEX's trips, contacted me by phone in 2012, explaining she had seen and read my book "Adventures of a 'Gringo' Researcher in Brazil in the 1960s." After a 45-minute telephone conversation which turned out to be an interview, she said we should go ahead and formalize it and welcomed me aboard.

I, not living in that world, had not heard of LEX, but soon discovered it was the premiere company in expedition trips throughout the seven seas, with a fleet of over a dozen expedition ships, the Explorer the flagship. The occasion would be the 125th Anniversary of National Geographic Magazine and at sea plus on shore stops along the entire east coast of South America, from Trinidad Tobago to Buenos Aires, featuring Brazil's entire eastern coast. I got on in Belém do Pará near the Amazon River, and from there the ship traveled to Fernando de Noronha, a UNESCO World Site, to Salvador da Bahia, Ilhéus in cacao country, Abrolhos and the Whale sightings, Rio de Janeiro, the resort town of Parati, The Paranaguá-Curtiba-Train to Morretes, and lastly, the Wildlife Preserve of TAIM near Rio Grande in Southern Brazil. We continued to Montevideo and a "gaucho" ranch and finally ended in cosmopolitan Buenos Aires seeing the capitol (think Juan and Eva Perón), the Cathedral (think Pope Francis), the San Telmo District (think Diego Maradona, Tango singer Carlos Gardel and tango performance.)

From the back cover:

"This book tells of Professor Curran's experiences on board this great expedition ship on the 2013 voyage. The book recounts early efforts to join with the ship crew, staff, and guest speakers in the collective task of providing an enriching experience for the guests or passengers. Secondly, it detail's Curran's contribution of speaking of Brazilian culture and preparing the guests for the places to be seen in that country. Finally, it details the trip itself: "At Sea" with the focus on educational talks by guest speakers and recaps by the naturalists and "On Shore" with cultural and historical vignettes of the place visited."

I add: the principal speakers, Wade Davis, Frank Lovejoy, and Jacob Edgar were/ are world renowned. I was a little fish in a very large pond, literally and figuratively. Crew and staff on the Explorer were no less impressive. And guests were astonishing in background and personal lives. I can't begin to restate here all the "goodies," but even a perusal of the table of contents tells much of the story.

19

A Professor Takes to the Sea II

2014. Brazil to Buenos Aires

2016 Atlantic Odyssey. Ushuaia, Argentina to Funchal, Madeira via Rio de Janeiro, Fernando de Noronha, Cabo Verde, and At Sea

Trafford Publishing, Bloomington, 2018, 357 pp.

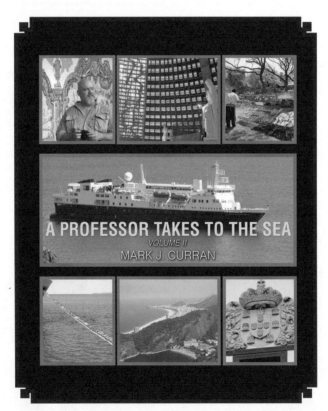

A Professor Takes to the Sea II

Volume II tells of two separate trips with some quirks and surprises. In all honesty neither trip had the brilliant cast of characters of that historic 2013 trip, but folks, it wasn't bad. There were still stars and super stars. From an A+ to A-. I was no longer a "rookie," but still ran into two or three glitches, one just for not being familiar with the DER (Daily Expedition Report) and the correct posting of it to the internet and all the protocol. No one explained, and it was a case of learn as you go.

Trip I in 2014 was planned soon after 2013 as I was invited aboard by Ralph the head LEX guy in charge of personnel; he wanted a quick answer (he gave me one week to decide). It was a compliment to the work in 2013. I would have been crazy not to take it. The 2014 trip all started with a "bizarre" event (as on-board historian David Barnes remarked): Explorer coming down from the Azores to Cabo Verde had a small situation: two or three passengers did not have up to date visas or other documents to continue on to South America, and one passenger lost his $$$ camera somewhere in the drink in the Atlantic. I was requested to take such documents and a new camera to the ship, but docked not in Brazil but in Cabo Verde just off the coast of West Africa. It enabled me to spend one night and day in Boston where I now could visit the Harvard Peabody Museum and see their famous exhibit on Maya Civilization and then get to an Irish Pub, plus fly across the Atlantic to the tiny country of Cabo Verde. After I froze in Cabo's super air-conditioned hotel and swam in their icy salt water swimming pool, Explorer arrived and now familiar routine ensued. Oh, except that I learned they would clean the ship thoroughly in the Atlantic crossing, the crew now dressed unbelievably casually instead of those smart Explorer Navy uniforms.

New faces (but old to LEX) were the EL (Expediton Leader) Jim Kelly an amazing oceanographer, and soon to be good friend Carlos Navarro the undersea diver. Carlos was from Mexico and did research on whales close to us in Phoenix, at Puerto Peñasco. We had great talks on Mexican history, anthropology and especially his M.A. thesis: the jaguar in northern Mexico and the Yucatán. Sissy Brimberg was chief photographer (her husband long time veteran Cotton whom I had met on the first trip in 2013, a victim drowning on a trip just months earlier.) Kike Calvo from Spain, major National Geographic photographer, and old friend of music fame Jacob Edgar were also aboard. One of the major guest speakers was Alberto Pfeifer from Brazil, an expert on geopolitics and Brazilian matters. He and his daughter Flora and I had wonderful conversations about all things Brazilian. I recall her favorite poet was Fernando Pessoa of Portugal.

I repeated many of the talks from the first expedition on various aspects of Brazil, we visited the same places in Brazil, and finished once again in Uruguay and Argentina. New experiences and especially new friendships were the high points of this trip.

Part II of this book details the final trip in 2016; the trip title was "Atlantic Odyssey 108," 54 degrees below and 54 above the equator from Ushuaia Argentina to Hamburg Germany. The original gist was to be mainly "at sea," an oceanic voyage with emphasis on specialists of the seas. We had a couple of surprises. The first for me was that by the hair on my chinny chin chin, I made the flight from Phoenix to Dallas. Old hat for LEX people, not for me. The problem was weather or traffic in Los Angeles where the flight was coming from, delays, delays, and cancellation of flights. I ended up running through the Dallas airport to make the international flight. LEX just said, "Let us know if you don't make the flight." What they did not say is that it would be impossible to make the date of departure of the ship in Argentina. End of story. End of trip!

Okay. I made it to Buenos Aires, joined the city tour (like in 2013 and 2014), we all hopped a local small jet for the several hour flight to cold, windy, snowy Ushuaia (the gateway to Antarctica) where Explorer was waiting. New naturalists were largely from Argentina, drinking mate herbal tea from their gourds with silver straws; they hung out up on the chart deck in the mornings. I got to know three or four of them; all were incredibly impressive for their knowledge of the South Atlantic, the Falklands, and all points south. One was a former fishing guide in Argentina and told stories of humongous trout and living with real "gauchos" ("we don't eat vegetables unless our women are around") and one a splendid horseman and naturalist. A major speaker was Roddy Bray from South Africa; not doubting his expertise which was astounding, but a bit of a puzzle because we had no destination near South Africa. They probably thought the same of me. I did the usual talks on Brazil in the beginning, but added a series on Portugal, Vasco da Gama, and Camões when we drew near to Madeira toward the very end of the trip.

Please see at least the table of contents (Amazon.com will show it) for all the amazing talks and highlights. I will mention only one or two: first the ship's engine propellers became entangled in a huge, mile long fishing line of a trawler, this just a day or two after departure. We had to stop at a port well south of Buenos Aires to have undersea divers go down and untangle the royal mess – result, the itinerary would be cut short, and we would dock in Madeira, not Hamburg, as the final stop.

I did get to do Brazil talks and lead a small group in adventurers in downtown Rio, but that was it until near Madeira. We stopped in Cabo Verde and saw the live impressive volcano but where one could also see the barrenness of the Island, the poverty and surmise indeed why so many of the natives have migrated to Boston and New England. By the way, I expected continental Portuguese but only heard "crioulo" which I could not understand at all.

After Cabo Verde on the way to Madeira they called on me for several talks, on Portugal, its history and culture, Vasco da Gama, and I threw in or made available an entire account of my travels in Portugal a few years ago.

Madeira to me for the first time was wonderful! Green, beautiful, and with an incredible fish and flower market downtown and better yet, its old Historical Center "O Largo do Município" with the Jesuit Church, the Funchal Botanical Gardens, and best of all, the whale museum in a nearby town. This was all new and fascinating.

LEX brought in a special airplane, from NIKI airlines in Germany, "irrigated" us all with copious amounts of Portuguese wine and flew us two or three hours to the original final destination of Hamburg. This was my only time in Germany and it is a blur - a night in a hotel, little sleep, then British Airways to London, Heathrow, and the transatlantic flight to Newark (I only remember the huge Budweiser Beer Sign on a building outside the terminal, Hasidic Jews bowing and praying near a window in the terminal, a night at a decent hotel where I watched major league baseball and then the five hour flight home to Phoenix. Whew!)

It is all in the large book in all its detail. Hopefully a reader or two will check it out. This ended my affiliation with LEX, alas, with problems in Brazil, they took it off their itinerary.

20

Letters from Brazil II – Research, Romance, and Dark Days Ahead. Trafford, 2019, 150 pp.

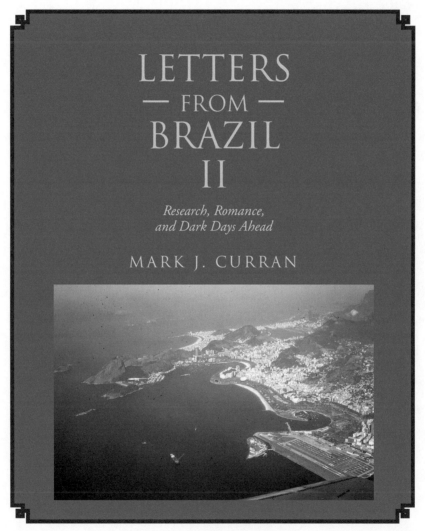

Letters from Brazil II

So now it is 2019 and I'm still trying to keep busy. "Letters II" came up, but someone evidently finding "Letters I" a bit dull, said, "Add more sex." Hmm. I did and found that two or three sections shocked some readers, including my daughter! Not my fault. It was an unmentioned person close to me who suggested spicing up the deal! No problem. No one will read it anyway. Here's the blurb on the back cover:

"Letters from Brazil II" is a continuation of "Letters from Brazil" in 2017. Mike Gaherty, now an assistant professor at the University of Nebraska in Lincoln, is back in Brazil to continue research and begin the battle for publication in a "publish or perish" academic world. He now has a Brazilian visa as a journalist-researcher in his role of writing occasional "Letters" to the New York Times International Section and is working in liaison with the Department of Research - Western Hemisphere Analysis of the U.S. State Department (INR – WHA). "Letters" will chronicle what he sees and experiences in Brazil – politics, economics, and especially daily life under the evolving military regime. The Brazilian Intelligence Agencies, the DOPS and the SNI, are aware of his role and keep constant surveillance of his activities. Life gets complicated as Mike juggles romantic interests both back at home and in Rio de Janeiro. And research evolves to treat the relationship between the folk – popular stories in verse ("literatura de cordel") and MPB (Brazilian Popular Music), especially regarding the composer, singer, and musician Chico Buarque de Hollanda and his efforts to write and perform in Brazil while battling with the generals' censorship laws under AI – 5. There are many surprises for Mike, some pleasurable, a few dangerous. Life for a researching professor turns out to be not as pedestrian as might be expected."

21

A Rural Odyssey – Living Can Be Dangerous. Trafford Publishing, Bloomington, 2019, 208 pp.

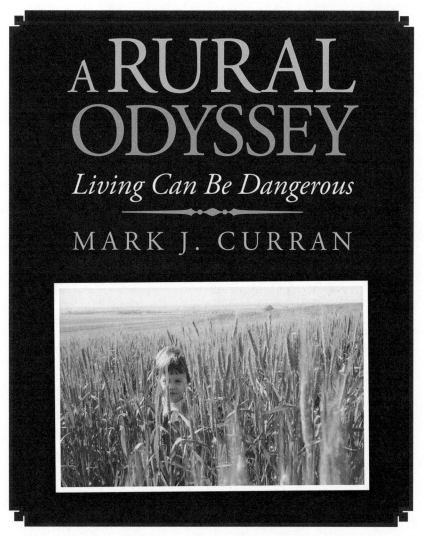

A Rural Odyssey – Living Can Be Dangerous

This book continues my early adventures into fiction, called my me "a cultural, historical narrative in fiction." Why? I can't sustain a short story or a novel but can write "vignettes" recreated from non – fiction. In this case I took "The Farm" and created fiction for those who did not read it (meaning most everyone). I did count fifteen episodes in the new book not in "The Farm." I had not thought about that until a good high school friend said he could not see where it was fiction. Ha! Read the book. I think a short synopsis is not out of order.

"A RURAL ODYSSEY – Living Can Be Dangerous" is the story of Mick O'Brien's growing up on a small wheat farm in Central Kansas in the 1940s and 1950s. It tells of his Irish American, Catholic, pioneering farm parents, the religious and moral beliefs of that tradition and the consequences of living out the same. Mick and his siblings inherit that tradition. Growing food, farm chores, raising and caring of livestock, field work om the tractor, and harvest provide the family subsistence, but not without danger. School, sports, fun with buddies, and imaginary games fill Mick's teen age years. Music, singing and the guitar, and a special musical friendship are an important chapter of that time with unplanned consequences. Unforeseen challenges and the unpredictable dangers of life fill the O'Brien's days as well. Work and play, joy, and sadness. Mick tells it all as it happened.

Alert: there is an interesting surprise ending!

22

Letters from Brazil III. From Glad Times to Sad Times.
Trafford Publishing, Blooming, 2019, 141 pp.

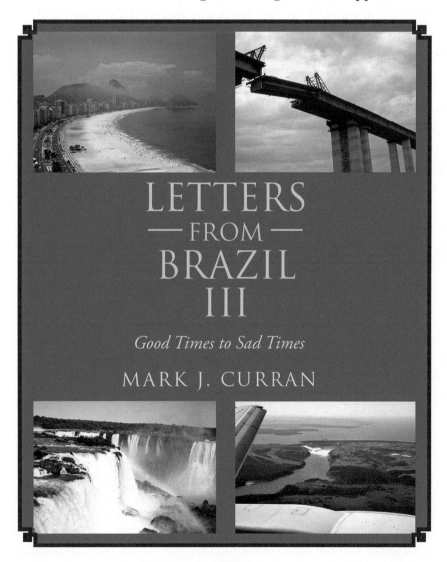

LETTERS
— FROM —
BRAZIL
III

Good Times to Sad Times

MARK J. CURRAN

Obviously, this book is a continuation of "Letters II;" I am now a bit more comfortable with my fictional narrative and it flows better. Here is the back cover blurb:

"Letters from Brazil III" is a continuation of Professor Mike Gaherty's adventures in Brazil. It chronicles in fiction Mike's initiation into the Portuguese-Brazilian academic world in the milieu of a major international "congress." The academic affair is followed by Mike's friendship and involvement with singer-composer Chico Buarque de Hollanda, the reporting for the New York Times of his songs jousting with Brazil's "prior censorship" board, and Mike's participation on one of Chico's LP's and successive concerts in São Paulo and Rio. The latter experience becomes dicey and dangerous with interference, surprising cooperation, and then bad times with the military regime's enforcement agency – the "Department of Public Security." Mike, still a bachelor, is entertained and then becomes enmeshed in fun times turned complicated with beautiful "carioca" women.

23

A Rural Odyssey II - Abilene - Digging Deeper, Trafford Publishing, Bloomington, 2020, 250 pp.

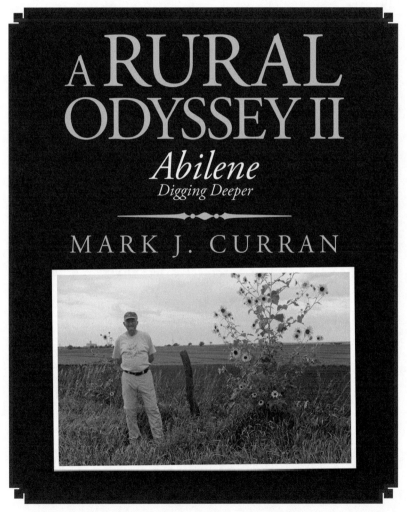

A Rural Odyssey II – Abilene – Digging Deeper

I am getting more familiar with fiction now and "Rural Odyssey II" is a big jump from the first volume based almost solely on the non-fiction "The Farm" with just fifteen moments fictionalized. In all modesty, there are some truly creative moments in II, in no small part due to a wonderful new character, Mike O'Brien's Jewish girl friend, Mariah Palafox, her family in Overland Park and her aunt and uncle in Mexico City where a segment of the narrative occurs. The book takes place in Abilene to be sure, but now changed, evolved and with some, uh, "adventure" possible. It is one of my personal favorites, a good "read" now and again, fun and even educational! Here is the blurb on the back cover:

"A RURAL ODYSSEY II – ABILENE – DIGGING DEEPER" is the continuation of the story of Mick O'Brien, now a college graduate and back in his hometown of Abilene, Kansas teaching at the new Junior College. He settles into daily life in Abilene and spends time with girlfriend Mariah Palafox a professor of English at the Juco. Family, friends, teaching, research, and work on Mick's "History of Abilene" take up most of his time. Mick and Mariah become close friends, then romantically involved. This leads to visits to her family and summer travel in Mexico and Spain, tips and hints aided by her relatives. Family ethnicity – Irish and Jewish – color the relationship. Life in Abilene gets dicey and dangerous with repercussions from previous problems with local criminals, then KKK activists and a return to violence and now larger threats to the citizens and town of Abilene.

24

Around Brazil on the 'International Adventurer' – A Panegyric in Fiction
Trafford Publishing, Bloomington, 2020, pp.

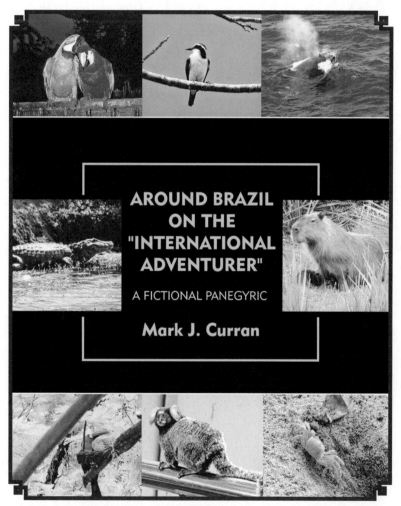

Around Brazil on the "International Adventurer"

So, I've caught a bit of the fiction "bug," partly out of necessity and partly by choice. First things first: enjoying an amazing retirement with talks and visits to Washington D.C. for the "Cordel" symposium at no less than the Library of Congress (2011), two visits to New York City for giving talks at the Brazilian Endowment of the Arts (2012 and 2017) and a fortuitous adventure on the National Explorer Ship in 2013, 2014 and 2016, that phase of talks, travel and adventure ended. I did the two books on the LEX experience, but now, what to do? Aha! Fictionalize the Explorer Trips!

Mike Gaherty now is working for "Adventure Travel" out of Los Angeles, assigned as cultural lecturer on their flagship, the "International Adventurer" for a 30-day trip from Manaus, Brazil to Buenos Aires in 1972. I borrowed heavily from the Explorer ship and experience, but changed all the names, added a romantic interest and a few fictitious episodes. The back cover "blurb" should cover it:

"Around Brazil on the 'International Adventurer' – a Fictional Panegyric" is the story of Professor Mike Gaherty in a new "gig" as Cultural Speaker for Adventure Travel's small ship expedition around Brazil, a thirty-day trip from Manaus in the Amazon Basin to Rio Grande in the South with major stops in Belém do Pará, Recife, Salvador, Ilhéus, Rio de Janeiro and Parati. Adventurers will experience nature on the entire trip, birds, animals, and plant life, but will be exposed to the history and culture of a good part of Brazil. The date is 1972 and the political undercurrent of Brazil's military regime and its battle against Leftist Subversion affects the expedition. This, however, is the old, fun, colorful, and entertaining Brazil of years past. Mike and his new colleagues of staff and crew of "Adventurer" mesh well, and there is time for an amorous relationship with Amy, the Assistant Adventure Leader on the ship. Surprises are in tow.

25

Pre – Columbian Mexico. Plans, Pitfalls, and Perils. Trafford Publishing, Bloomington, 2020. 182 pp.

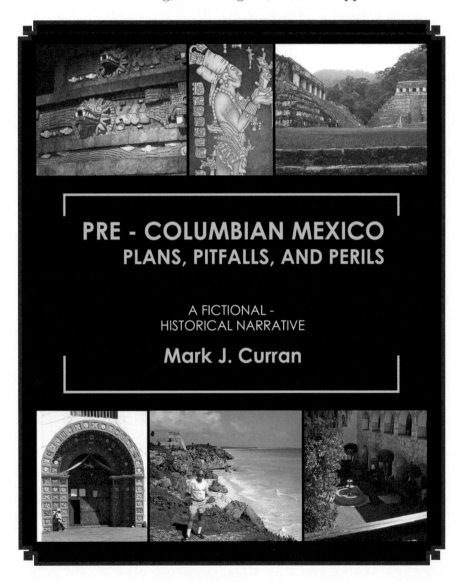

I enjoyed writing "Around Brazil" so much that I decided to do a second book in the same fashion, this time "Adventure Travel" in Mexico. The time is summer 1974. Mike and Amy. The book borrows heavily from material taught in classes at ASU for some thirty years: Pre – Columbian culture in Mexico and modern cities and places near the old archeological sites. But adventure is afoot! Mike and Amy run into some shady and then bad characters that perhaps allow the reader to actually finish the book! And scrapes and close calls abound. Our heroes are now in love and hope to live to tell about it. The back cover blurb:

"Pre – Columbian Mexico – Plans, Pitfalls and Perils" is historical fiction and continues the adventures and escapades of Professor Mike Gaherty, this time along with colleague – girlfriend Amy Carrier, on a travel, research trip to Mexico. The goal is to scope out and research Mexico for a possible Adventure Travel Expedition, its first all on land, and in partnership with New York Times Travel. Surprises come, unexpected opposition to foreign tourism and travel in Mexico. Mike and Amy are haunted by vestiges of Pre – Columbian gods, peoples, and places."

Other than the fiction, the most important part, one returns to the following towns, cities and archeological sites in Mexico:

Mexico City: The National Museum of History and Anthropology

Teotihuacán

Monte Albán, Mitla (Oaxaca)

Palenque (San Cristóbal de las Casas, San Juan Chamula, Água Azul)

Las Ventas (Villa Hermosa)

Uxmal, Chichén Itzá (Mérida, Cancún, Tulum)

26

"Portugal and Spain on the 'International Adventurer.'"
Trafford Publishing, Bloomington, 2020, 202 pp.

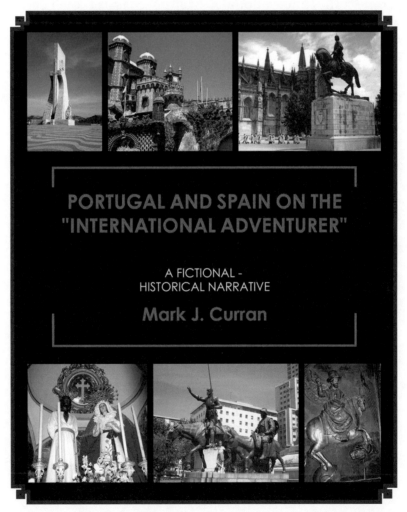

PORTUGAL AND SPAIN ON THE
"INTERNATIONAL ADVENTURER"

A FICTIONAL -
HISTORICAL NARRATIVE

Mark J. Curran

Portugal and Spain on the "International Adventurer"

Mike and Amy now combine the "International Adventurer" and land travel to Portugal and Spain on their third venture for Adventure Travel. The reader is now familiar with the crew and staff of IA from Portugal. Several interesting travelers are on board, and adventures ensue. The back cover blurb:

"Portugal and Spain on the 'International Adventurer'" is historical fiction and continues the travel adventures of Professor Mike Gaherty with IA "Assistant Adventure Leader" Amy Carrier and a volatile cast of fictional adventurers traversing Portugal and Spain. One sees the best of these two off and on enemies and competitive nations – monuments, Literary Personages, food, and wine, and "Pousadas" and "Paradores." Travel, controversy, and dangerous moments from post – Salazar and post – Franco days ensue."

Real life travel for the author is the basis for the important historical and cultural sites to be seen. In Portugal: Madeira, Lisbon, Sintra, Nazaré, Alcobaça, Óbidos, Fátima, Batalha, O Porto, Coimbra, Santiago de Compostela, and the Algarve. In Spain: Málaga, Córdoba, Granada, Sevilla, Valencia, Madrid, Toledo, León, Burgos, the Basque Country, Zaragoza and a surprise ending in Barcelona.

27

Rural Odyssey III – Dreams Fulfilled and Back to Abilene.
Trafford Publishing, Bloomington, 2021, 206 pp.

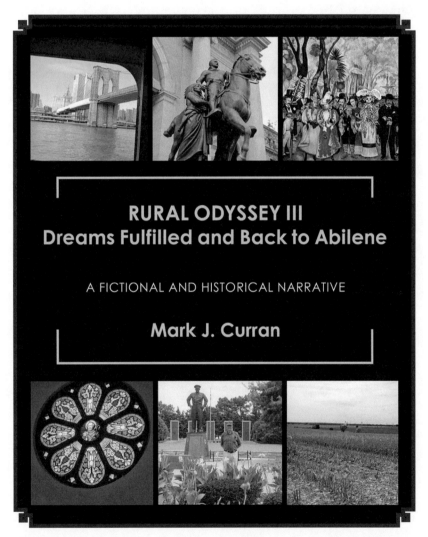

Rural Odyssey III – Dreams Fulfilled and back to Abilene

Mike and Mariah make the decision to return to the East and pursue advanced degrees to create a possible bettering of teaching positions and academic success in the future. Mike begins a Ph.D. program at Brown University in Providence Rhode Island in Spanish, Latin American Studies, and Luso-Brazilian studies. The reasons are the presence of America's best scholar of political science on matters of Brazil, Professor Thomas Skidmore, and Brown's excellent staff for Portuguese language and Brazil. Mariah is accepted into the School of Law at Harvard in Boston. Proximity allows them to continue the romance.

After three years of study both return to Mexico for research on the respective dissertations, Mike investigating Mexican folk – popular culture in the "corridos," the engravings of José Guadalupe Posada, and art of Diego Rivera and Frida Kahlo, Mariah studying the Mexican System of Education and the role of the "traditional female rural schoolteachers" and the evolution of the same today.

They return to Abilene and the Dwight D. Eisenhower College, both full – time teachers and administrators, manage to complete the degrees, and live life in Abilene. The culmination is that romance turns into marriage celebrated in festive fashion on the old family farm with all the relatives and friends present. Mariah's Jewish background melds with Mike's evolved Catholicism in a combined liturgical event. Jewish and Catholic custom abide with fun for all.

28

The Collection. Trafford Publishing, Bloomington, 2021, 308 pp.

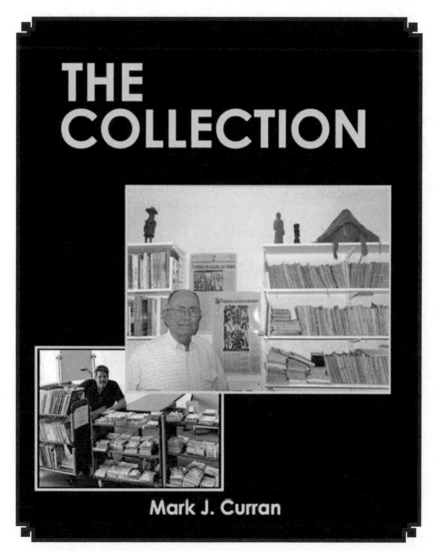

The Collection

In 2020 I am almost twenty years into the first "official retirement" and all the books already seen. One begins to think of the future, that is, if something happens to me, incapacitates me or worse, what would my wife or daughter do with those few thousand "cordel" broadsides on the shelves of my office in Mesa, Arizona, or for that matter, the two shelves of primary sources collected over all the years? What ensued was an accident of sorts. I had done another book and thought it might be of interest to professors of Portuguese and Brazilian Studies. I got on the website of BRASA, the national Brazilian Studies Association and recognized a name, Professor Chris Dunn, the President of BRASA.

Chris and I met by chance at the BRASA meeting in Recife in 2000, he a youngster recently graduated from Brown and beginning a career at Tulane. I wrote Chris asking for information to publicize a book on the BRASA newsletter, he answered with enthusiasm. A few months later Chris wrote an e-mail from Tulane, noting he had seen my "Retrato do Brasil em Cordel" in the Latin American Library and was highly complementary of the book. In an afterthought he asked me what plans I had for my collection. I must add a paragraph.

In 2011 after participating in the wonderful seminar on "Cordel" at the Library of Congress in Washington, like a good researcher, I spent a few intense hours perusing just the titles from the LOC archives, perhaps ten to twelve thousand broadsides. It was then that I began to think of offering my collection to the LOC. But other considerations came into play, this of interest to anyone involved with "Cordel." First, the LOC collection was excellent and had most, not all, of what I collected. They would really gain little from me. And I thought: if a young student wanted to come to Washington, D.C. to consult the archives, how in the world would he or she afford the stay in that city? Secondly, I always had the perhaps romantic idea of donating it all to some entity in Brazil, as my talk in 2011 was titled "A Debt to Repay."

The truth is the great public collection in Brazil, that of the Fundação Casa de Rui Barbosa, had far more broadsides than I and mine would only replicate part of it. The best private collection in Brazil, the Átila de Almeida Collection was housed at the University of Paraíba in Campina Grande, in safe hands, i.e. the library climate controlled and reasonably exempt from pilfering and theft. I had heard from the most important of Brazilian scholars and collectors, Manuel Diégues Júnior and Ariano Suassuna among others, that their donated collections had simply "disappeared" over time, few details, but thievery and whatever. These are the reasons I no longer considered Brazil as a destination, pure and simple.

So, the outstanding Latin American Library at Tulane, exemplary in all the factors already discussed, became my choice. Another matter, I had strongly considered Tulane for graduate school or job possibilities in past years, so had an affinity for the place. Chris put me in touch with Professor Hortensia Calvo at the Library, an agreement was reached, and in the spring of 2021 the transfer was made. Incidentally, the Library has a limited number of "scholarships" to house prospective researchers. I have absolutely no regrets. There are four blank shelves in my home library, intentionally kept empty, to remind me what was there. Any research or writing since has been done via sources from the Internet and new technology. I have dozens of photos and a few dozen broadsides I kept as "souvenirs." And of course, all the research and resulting books reported here.

A few months after the transaction and packing and shipping of the books, it occurred to me to write my own "official" record of it all. "The Collection" is that book. In Part 1 I once again tell of the collecting from 1966 to 2005, recounting the poets I met, purchases from them, the famous "barracas" de "cordel" of Edson Pinto in Recife and others, and the "odisséia" of collecting over the years, all through the Northeast in 1966, later in Bahia and especially Rio de Janeiro later, and then importantly through the mail for over thirty years. Vignettes of collection, stories of the poets, the publishers and the places are all recorded together with photos of most of them.

The book tells of onsite collecting in 1966-1967, 1969, 1978, 1981, 1990, 1996, 2001, 2002 and finally 2005. A few dozen poets, the "greats" of the 1960s and beyond are noted. See the book.

Part II is the large portion of the book. The titles of perhaps 3000 broadsides, titles of important xeroxes of major works of "cordel" over the years, and titles from collecting through the mail are all there in over 180 pp. of manuscript. Then the bibliography of my entire "cordel" secondary works library follows.

My idea was and is that a prospective, serious researcher at Tulane could use this book as a first guide to the collection.

I am compelled to list poets and publishers named:

Edson Pinto, José Bento da Silva, José Francisco Campos, João José da Siva, José Soares, Manoel Camilo dos Santos, Manoel Caboclo e Silva, José Bernardo da Silva, Mário Brito, Joaquim Batista de Sena, José Costa Leite, Rodolfo Coelho Cavalcante, Cuíca de Santo Amaro, Minelvino Francisco Silva, Erotildes Miranda dos Santos, João José dos Santos (Azulão), Apolônio Alves dos Santos, Gonçalo Ferreira da Silva, Franklin Maxado, Raimundo Santa Helena, Antônio Oliveira, J. Borges, Abraão Batista, Téo Azevedo, Marcelo Soares, Varneci Nascimento, José Alves Sobrinho, Klevisson and Arievaldo Viana.

And the masters from the old publishers: Francisco das Chagas Batista, Leandro Gomes de Barros, and others of their era.

Xeroxes from the Fundação Casa de Rui Barbosa, the Orígenes Lessa Collection, the "Núcleo de Pesquisa da Literatura de Cordel" in Bahia, the "Biblioteca da Literatura de Cordel" from the Universide Federal da Paraíba, the Átila de Almeida Collection from the man and his library in Campina Grande, Paraíba, from the "Fundos Villa-Lobos" at the "Institute de Estudos Brasileiros" of the Universidade de São Paulo, and a lesser extent from the "Campanha de Folclore" of Rio de Janeiro and the National Library in Rio de Janeiro.

29

Letters from Brazil IV. Trafford Publishing, Bloomington, 2021,155 pp.

MARK J. CURRAN

LETTERS
— FROM —
BRAZIL
IV

A Time to Hope

Letters from Brazil II – A Time to Hope

This is the final in the series "Letters from Brazil." It began with baby steps in fiction and now has evolved to more fiction, yet with episodes based now and again on my forays to Brazil from 1966 to 2013. In a sense, it is a "goodbye" to this thread of writings. The back cover blurb says it best:

"Letters from Brazil IV" is the most recent in the series of Professor Mike Gaherty's travel and research in Brazil. He has returned in 1984 after an "invited" hiatus since 1971 by the General heading Brazil's "Pre – Censorship Board," this due to Mike's friendship, research, collaboration with, and defense of singer – composer Chico Buarque de Hollanda. Mike is reporting on current events and politics for the International Section of the "New York Times," in liaison with the Institute of International Research, Latin America Sector. The includes the volatile climate of "Direct Elections Now" for the presidency. He is shadowed by the DOPS (the Brazilian Security Agency) but has become great friends with the Captain in charge of keeping an eye on him. Mike renews many old friendships and finds time to update his research specialty The "Literatura de Cordel" as folk – popular journalism since censorship ended in 1979. He also must maneuver between some and sidestep other former romantic liaisons in Brazil. Further collaboration in a Chico Buarque concert and dealing with Brazilian security forces gets dicey. Brazilian literature, religion, music, food, and his own nostalgia for "Black Orpheus" complete the adventure.

30

The Master of the "Literatura de Cordel" – Leandro Gomes de Barros. A Bilingual Anthology of Selected Works, Trafford Publishing, Bloomington, 2022, 220 pp.

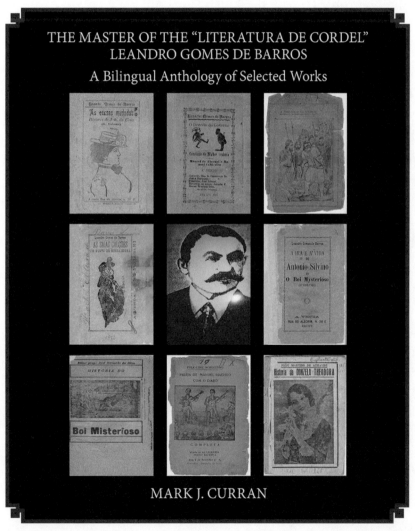

The Master of the "Literatura de Cordel" – Leandro Gomes de Barros

This book marks a return to the academic: the topic of the original Ph.D. dissertation of 1968, Brazil's "literatura popular em verso" and features its most important poet, Leandro Gomes de Barros. Two major factors brought about the endeavor: the digitization of all of Leandro's extant works by the personnel in the research section of the Fundação Casa de Rui Barbosa in Rio, and equally important, the passage of time allowing all of Leandro's works to be in the public domain, i.e. no hassles about copyright. Here is the blurb from the back cover:

"The Master of the 'Literatura de Cordel' – Leandro Gomes de Barros. A Bilingual Anthology of Selected Works" is Professor Curran's return to research and writing from his first days in Brazil in 1966 -1967 on a Fulbright – Hays Fellowship for Ph.D. dissertation work. This book treats "cordel's" best known and arguably best poet, a translation to English of his selected works, and a commentary on his pioneering days of the "Literatura de Cordel." Among the poet's topics were the changing times, foreigners in Brazil, government – politics – and war, mothers – in – law, sugar cane rum, religion and satire, banditry, the oral poetic duel, and the long, narrative poems from the European popular tradition. Curran in addition gives a synopsis of the "Literatura de Cordel" as it was in its heyday in his initial research in the 1960s. The translation was a challenge but also a great pleasure.

"Adventure Travel" in Guatemala - The Maya Heritage. Trafford Publishing, 2022, 160 pp.

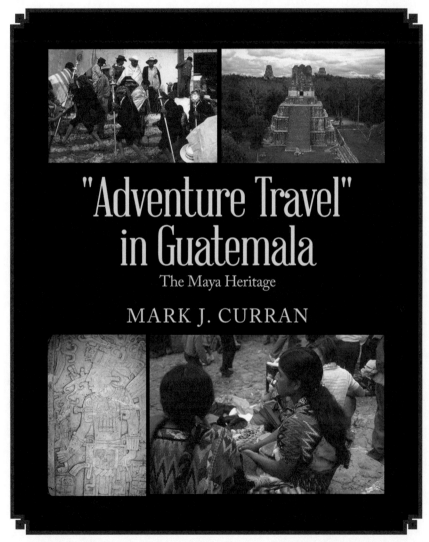

"Adventure Travel" in Guatemala – The Maya Heritage

This is the latest in the "Adventure Travel" series following narratives on Brazil, Mexico, Portugal and Spain. It combines history, culture of the Mayas and Professor Curran's past travel in Guatemala with an added experiment in fiction. The back cover "blurb" is as follows:

"'Adventure Travel' in Guatemala – The Maya Heritage" is the fourth in the series of fiction – travel – culture – adventure books on Brazil, Mexico, Portugal and Spain, and now Guatemala. Professor Mike Gaherty and AT Leader Amy Carrier are in Guatemala researching that country as a destination for a future AT Travel Trip for its "Adventurers." They investigate Antigua, Puerto San José, El Lago de Atitlán, Chichicastenango, and Tikal in Guatemala and Copán in Honduras, checking out the history and culture of both the Spanish and Maya Heritages. Emphasis however is on the Maya people, their lives and efforts to survive under adverse circumstances in post 1976 earthquake and political turmoil in Guatemala. There are surprises and dangerous moments for Mike and Amy, and difficult decisions for AT Travel.

32

TWO by Mark J. Curran. ASU Days. The Guitars a Music Odyssey.
Trafford Publishing, Bloomington, 2022, 226 pp.

TWO by Mark J. Curran

Book I ASU Days tells the story beginning with graduate study for the Ph.D. in Spanish and Latin American Studies and the account of Mark's years at Arizona State University. It is comprised of memories of teaching and research days at ASU but also a description of campus life dating to 1968.

Book II The Guitars – A Music Odyssey recounts the role of music in Mark's life from age 14 in 1955 to the present. The main characters are the guitars: a simple steel-stringed Stella in 1955, an electric Kay and amplifyer in high school, 1955-1959 and college days, a Sears-Roebuck Catalogue Classic at the same time, a Brazilian Rosewood Classic from Rio de Janeiro in 1966 and a Manuel Rodríguez Classic from Madrid, clcctrificd for performance, 2002. The study, learning, practice and performing range from early Pop and Rock n' Roll from Elvis Presley days, to serious home study of classic guitar, to the folk tunes of the 1960s, Classic Country and Western, Irish, "O' Brother Where Art Thou" and Classic Guitar and Contemporary Catholic Songs for meditation at church. The final chaper is a work in progress: practice and performance at home.

33

RURAL ODYSSEY IV – PARALLELS. Abilene – Cowboys – "Cordel." Trafford Publishing, Bloomington, 2023, 227 pp.

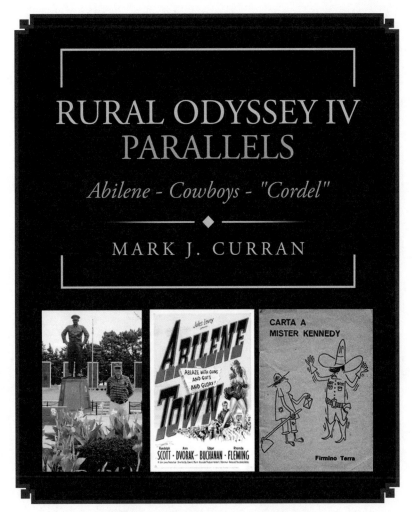

Rural Odyssey IV - Parallels

RURAL ODYSSEY IV PARALLELS. Abilene – Cowboys – "Cordel" is a return to the Rural Odyssey series, a narrative in fiction telling of Professor Mike O'Brien's work on a "History of Abilene," life with his young wife, Mariah Palafox O'Brien, and their jobs at DDEC (Dwight D. Eisenhower College) in Abilene. After telling of his "History of Abilene," the book recounts Mike and Mariah's trip to Brazil in the summer of 1971 via Fulbright Lecture Grants. Mike gives talks on Eisenhower, Abilene and the Cowboy days and "cordel," and Mariah lectures on American Literature. "The Great Gatsby," "The Sound and the Fury," and "To Kill a Mockingbird" are a few highlights. They meet important military, literary, and folkloric figures in Rio de Janeiro, São Paulo, Bahia and Recife and visit Brazil's famous tourist and cultural sites as well. Mike's Catholic and Mariah's Jewish heritages come into play.

34

The Writing and Publishing Journey. Trafford Publishing, Bloomington, 2023, 153 pp.

ADDENDUM: ARTICLES OR CHAPTERS IN BOOKS

The following list is taken from the "Curriculum Vitae," a required record providing proof of one's efforts and work in the Academy. Each of these small texts has a story to tell as well. Some I scarcely remember writing; others marked very important memories in the teaching – writing – publishing years. They were all included in the boxes of materials sent to the Latin American Library at Tulane University in 2021. They can gather dust there just as well as on the shelves of the home office in Mesa, Arizona. The Trafford books already seen may be more interesting to some readers. I will take the time and energy to make brief comments on the more important items.

1969; "Influência da Literatura de Cordel na Literatura Brasileira". <u>Revista Brasileira de Folclore</u>. Rio de Janeiro, Instituto Nacional de Folclore, set. 1969, 3-15.

> This is the first published article and at a very good place. The "Brazilian Review of Folklore" was the best of its kind in 1969. The study basically is a chapter from the dissertation. The topic of major erudite authors in Brazil adapting works from "cordel" to their works will be of major importance in years to come. Studies on Ariano Suassuna, Jorge Amado and João Guimarães Rosa are cases in point. The article was welcomed by no less than Vicente Salles, the magazine's director, and later the same for the national CULTURA Magazine out of the new capital Brasília. We became friends in Rio and talked much of classical music and his wife's role as a violinist in the then National Symphony in Rio.

1971. Curran, Mark J. "Introduction and Selected Bibliography of History and Politics in Brazilian Popular Poetry." <u>Special Series</u>. Tempe: Center for Latin American Studies, 1971, 26 pp.

This is a "home grown" article published in a monograph at ASU. The topic is significant however, the germ for what years later would be the major book in Brazil - "História do Brasil em Cordel" already seen.

1972. "A Página Editorial do Poeta Popular". <u>Revista Brasileira de Folclore</u>. Rio de Janeiro, Instituto Nacional do Folclore, abril de 1972, 5-16.

This is the second article in the folklore magazine. It treats the back covers of the cordelian broadsides from early times in the 1920s to the 1960s. In effect, the back cover served as "the editorial page" for comments and opinions of the poets or just as likely the "advertising page" giving pertinent information on price, location of the printer and general editorial comments. Manoel Camilo dos Santos was the "king" of such statements, when he would rail against "thieves" stealing or plagiarizing his poems. He threatened to take them all to court by virtue of his "stable of lawyers." Not really.

1973a. "A Sátira e a Crítica Social na Literatura de Cordel". <u>Literatura Popular em Verso</u>. Estudos I. Rio de Janeiro: Fundação Casa de Rui Barbosa, 1973, 271-330. (With studies by Ariano Suassuna, Bráulio do Nascimento, Dulce Martins, Mark J. Curran, Manuel Diégues Júnior, Raquel de Queiróz and Sebastião Nunes Batista.) 1a edição, Rio, 1973. 2a. ed. Belo Horizonte: Itatiaia - USP, 1986.

I already treated this study, important in content as well as career advancement. It appeared in the book already mentioned, "Literatura Popular em Verso: Estudos I" by the Fundação Casa de Rui Barbosa in 1973 and granted my humble presence at a young age in the company of famous Brazilian writers and scholars of "cordel."

1973b. "The Journalistic Page of the Brazilian Popular Poet." <u>Arizona Latin American Conference on Latin American Studies</u>. Tempe: CLAS, 1973, 30-52.

This is the English version of the second article at the "Revista Brasileira de Folclore." The case is once again a modest monograph at the ASU Center for Latin American Studies.

1973c. "Jorge Amado" and "Ariano Suassuna", <u>A Dictionary of Brazilian Authors</u>. Eds. David Foster and Roberto Reis. Tempe: CLAS, 1973, 2-4, 141-142.

This is a very modest contribution to the "Dictionary." Tempe, CLAS again.

1975. "Twentieth Century Brazilian Literature: Influence of the Poetry of the Masses (Mário de Andrade, Jorge Amado, João Guimarães Rosa and Ariano Suassuna). <u>U.C.L.A. Semana de Arte Moderna Symposium</u>. Los Angeles, 1975, 146-159.

This is a "local" publication in Los Angeles, the papers from the symposium at U.C.L.A., but is important at least in two ways: the topic is the "seed" for larger studies on the influence of the "Literatura de Cordel" on Brazilian erudite authors (already treated in the books section). But equally important was the opportunity to meet some renowned scholars on Brazil who would play a role in the future academic career, E. Bradford Burns the Historian and Claude Hulet of Portuguese and Brazilian Literature at UCLA are cases in point. There were others from West Coast Schools as well.

1976. "Rodolfo Coelho Cavalcante: Brazilian Popular Poet and Propagandist of the <u>Literatura de Cordel</u>." <u>Proceedings of the Pacific Coast Council of Latin American Studies</u>. V. 5, 1976, 11-24.

My first published article on one of the major figures of all time of the "Literatura de Cordel," seen in the books section. But like the UCLA meeting, this was the first time I would meet and interact with West Coast professors of Latin American Studies, Roger Cuniff of San Diego State Publisher of the "Proceedings" for one, and I would become a "regular" over the years at the PCCLAS. As mentioned somewhere, my Ph.D. study and personal tastes were more attuned to area studies than literary theory, as well as the classes taught at ASU. The Council truly filled the bill.

1976b. "A Cultura Popular e Grande Sertão: Veredas." University of Southern California Symposium on Luso-Brazilian Oral Traditions: Verse Forms. Ed. Joanne Purcell, Los Angeles, USC, 1976, 36-81.

Once again, a local production of USC, this is the study I did sitting at a camp table in a cabin on Grand Mesa in Colorado in a frosty, frozen June of 1972. From such modest beginnings, the talk at USC, and then in Portuguese at a major international congress in Rio de Janeiro in 1973, a hiatus, in the "drawer" for years, an entry into a contest at the Fundação Casa de Rui Barbosa in 1985, and finally publication in Brazil/Brasil at Brown in 1995, perhaps no other research, writing, has gone through this journey. Let me count the ways: 23 years!

1976c. "An Annotated Bibliography of Selected Works on Brazil' Literatura de Cordel." Proceedings of the Pacific Coast Council of Latin American Studies. V. 5, 1976, 160-168.

I have little recall of this article since I do not normally do bibliographies, but I must have put together some of the major works. A local publication of conference proceedings by PCCLAS.

1978, "The Poetry of the Cangaço." Arizona Latin American Conference Papers. Tempe, CLAS, 1978, 24 pp.

Another local publication from the ASU Latin American Center, but the topic would get big play in future studies in Brazil.

1979. "From the <u>Cantador</u> to the <u>Poeta Popular</u>: The Folk-Popular Poetry of Northeastern Brazil." <u>Latin American Digest</u>. 13:4 (1979), 1-3, 20.

It was an overview of oral and written folk popular poetry. Minor in scope.

1980. "<u>Literatura de Cordel</u> Today: The Poets and the Publishers." <u>Journal of Latin American Lore</u>. 6:1 (1980), 55-75.

This is a lengthy article in a very respected journal; it was the result of written interviews with forty poets and publishers in Brazil in 1979. An important document.

1982. "Brazil's <u>Literatura de Cordel</u>: Its Distribution and Adaptation to the Brazilian Mass Market." <u>Studies in Latin American Popular Culture</u>. V. 1, 1982, 164-178.

This is the first of many published short studies for the major journal of its type in the U.S., that is, Latin American Popular Culture. It deals with the nuts and bolts of how the broadsides of "cordel" are currently published, distributed, and sold in Brazil.

1983. "Folk-Popular Literature in Brazil: a Seminal Study of "Stories on a String." <u>Studies in Latin American Popular Culture</u>. V.2, 1983, 234-238.

This is a rare book review but on an important topic: Candace Slater's important book on the "Literatura de Cordel," one of the best of its kind.

1984. "Politics in the Brazilian <u>Literatura de Cordel</u>: the View of Rodolfo Coelho Cavalcante." <u>Studies in Latin American Popular Culture</u>. Eds. Harold Hinds, Charles M. Tatum. V. 3, 1984, 115-126.

Once again, a good article in an important journal, this is early study and writing about Rodolfo, one of the most important and influential of poets-publishers of "cordel" for forty years in Brazil. The material will contribute to my book on Rodolfo in 1986 in Brazil.

1986. "The Brazilian Democratic Dream: The View from <u>Cordel</u>." <u>Luso-Brazilian Review</u>. 23:2 (1986), 29-46.

> I am having more luck with the major journals; the **LBR** is the best of its kind on topics to do with Brazil. The article topic is the battle for a return to democracy in Brazil in the "Eleições Diretas" campaign in 1984 and how "cordel" reported it all. Tancredo Neves would become the first democratically elected president in Brazil in 21 years in 1985.

1987. "Images of the United States in Brazil's <u>Literatura de Cordel</u>." <u>Proceedings of the Pacific Coast Council of Latin American Studies.</u> A paper read at the conference. 14:1 (1987), 145-172.

> I don't recall which images appear, but it is lengthy.

1988. "New <u>Cordel</u> in Brazil: 1985." <u>Studies in Latin American Popular Culture</u>, V. 7, 1988, 107-120.

> A good journal and new material garnered from research in Brazil in 1985.

1991. "<u>Cordel</u>: One Hundred Years of Brazilian History." <u>Brazil Hoje</u> (May-June, 1991) 1,9.

> The theme is important, I suspect early work on what will become a major book already treated, "História do Brasil em Cordel." The thesis is not that "cordel" is history, or popular history, but is an important source for those who do write history.

1991b. "A literatura de cordel: antes e agora." Special Portuguese Edition of <u>Hispania</u> (74:3) Sept. 1991, 570-576.

> Once again my work is now reaching the best of the academic journals in my field. The article received significant readership and reallly provided both an introduction and an update to the phenomonon in Brazil in 1991.

1995. "Grande Sertão: Veredas e a Literatura de Cordel." Brasil/ Brazil n. 14, ano 8, 1995, 9-49.

I wrote extensively of this long article in the book section. Jogging the memory, it broke new ground in relating the substratem topics of "cordel" to the same in what was Brazil's major novel at that time. The study won a prize in Brazil in 1985 and was the lead article in Brown's prestigious "Brasil/Brazil" Journal.

1996, "Brazil's Literatura de Cordel [String Literature]: Poetic Chronicle and Popular History." Studies in Latin American Popular Culture v. 15, 1996, 219-229.

My final article in this important journal, combining "cordel's" function of both folk-popular narrative poetry and Brazilian History.

Two or three more articles would appear in the proceedings of conferences in Brazil, but now all energy would be spent on the final academic books with great success in Brazil: "História do Brasil em Cordel" (1998) and "Retrato do Brasil em Cordel" (2010), both treated in the books section.

CONCLUSION

It is 2023. If my guardian angel keeps watching over me, and "the crick don't rise" (as we used to say in Kansas), more book titles may come. Right now, just fuzzy ideas in mind are:

"Adventure Travel" in Colombia. Moments of Mayhem

"Corridos y Cordel"

Rural Odyssey V – Mike and Mariah. A Return to Abilene or The Ticket Out East

"Cartas do Brasil" Mark J. Curran with Roberto Froelich

ABOUT THE AUTHOR

Mark Curran is a retired professor from Arizona State University where he worked from 1968 to 2011. He taught Spanish and Portuguese and their respective cultures. His research specialty was Brazil and its "popular literature in verse" or the "Literatura de Cordel," and he has published many articles in research reviews and now some fourteen books related to the "Cordel" in Brazil, the United States and Spain. The other books come from teaching topics at ASU and adventures in retirement years, now experimenting with fiction.

Professor Curran lives in Mesa, Arizona, and spends part of the year in Colorado. He is married to Keah Runshang Curran, and they have one daughter Kathleen who lives in Albuquerque, New Mexico, married to teacher Courtney Hinman in 2018. Her documentary film "Greening the Revolution" was presented most recently in the Sonoma Film Festival in California, this after other festivals in Milan, Italy, and New York City. Katie was named best female director in the Oaxaca Film Festival in Mexico.

The author's e-mail address is: profmark@asu.edu

His website address is: www.currancordelconnection.com

Printed in the United States
by Baker & Taylor Publisher Services